THE COMPLETE BOOK OF ELK HUNTING

Tips and Tactics for All Weather and Habitat Conditions

A ROCKY MOUNTAIN ELK FOUNDATION BOOK

SAM CURTIS

The Lyons Press
Guilford, Connecticut
An imprint of The Globe Pequot Press

The Lyons Press is an imprint of The Globe Pequot Press.

Printed in the United States of America

10 9 8 7 6 5 4 3 2 1

Library of Congress Cataloging-in-Publication Data

CONTENTS

Contents

INTRODUCTION

Certain elk hunts lodge in your memory because they are reminders of what hunting can be at its best. I recall, for example, a crystal-cold morning in Montana when I set off on foot in the dark to reach the top of a south-facing draw by daybreak. A light skiff of snow had fallen overnight, and the temperature was in the low teens. I guessed that any elk in the area would have remained under the protective cover of north-slope timber that night, but then might move onto the grassy south slopes for warmth and food by first light.

My hunch was right. The fresh elk tracks were there in the snow, including a large set that appeared to belong to a bull, but the elk themselves were a few steps ahead of me. The tracks angled up through timber that I knew thinned into a grassy swale just below the divide a half mile above. It was still early enough that the elk would probably be looking for food, at least for maybe an hour longer. But then they'd probably seek the security of the steep slope and thick downfall on the east side of the divide, a spot that would be very difficult to hunt.

Instead of following the tracks, I made a wide detour to reach the divide below the point where I thought the elk might cross. For another half hour I still-hunted toward that spot, staying below the ridgeline so I wouldn't be silhouetted against the sky. At last, a cow elk appeared in the sparse timber below. Then another. I waited motionless for long minutes, my firing position steadied by a fallen log. When the bull appeared, he was a good 150 yards up the ridge, aloof from the rest of the small herd and heading for the safety of the east slope. I figured I had a 10-yard window in which the bull would be in my sights. Luckily, he was walking.

The bullet entered just behind his shoulder, and he ran and rolled 50 yards down the east slope before coming to rest against an uprooted fir. Getting the quartered elk back up to the top of the divide was a bear of a job, which I refused to complain about. The rest of the hunt had unfolded the way I'd worked years for a hunt to unfold.

"Work" is the operative word here. To work at an elk hunt means knowing the habitat you're hunting and knowing what behavior to expect of the elk that use that habitat. It also means knowing the effects of weather, both long and short term, on the ways of elk. And it ultimately means tying your hunting tactics to what you know about those habits, habitats, and the weather. Working to make a hunt successful may even hinge on such subtle matters as knowing how logging practices and forest fires affect elk whereabouts.

The work of elk hunting is an ongoing process. It starts with your own observations and field experience—if you're lucky enough to live in elk country. It includes listening to and questioning experienced elk hunters and hunting guides. And, if you really want to work at preparing yourself for successful hunting, you can find a professional elk researcher, someone like Terry Lonner, whose name you'll see often in these pages, and ask him to tell you all he knows about these magnificent creatures.

You can also read the chapters ahead to learn about hunting elk, and I hope you won't consider it work. In *The Complete Book of Elk Hunting* I've combined my own thirty years of observations and hunting experience with the advice of other elk hunters and guides and the professional findings of elk biologists to bring you my perspective on the "work" of successful elk hunting. I've wrapped this advice in specific anecdotes from my own experiences. Hopefully, all of this will give you a good start on your first, or next, elk-hunting adventure.

Make no mistake. Elk hunting is the big league of big-game hunting. These are large, far-ranging animals. They can and will lead you well off the beaten track. In fact, you shouldn't launch into an elk hunt without some basic deer-hunting experience, including knowledge of the anatomy of a clean kill and some hands-on experience with field dressing big game. You need to know what to wear to keep warm and dry. You need to know how to keep from getting lost.

Assuming that readers have this basic grounding in woodsmanship and hunting, I have focused on the intricacies of elk habits, habitats, and changing environmental influences. Most of my hunting examples come from Montana, but the principles I discuss will prepare you for the work of elk hunting from New Mexico to Canada.

Sam Curtis
Bozeman, Montana

Recognizing
Habitats

Chapter 1

NATURAL HISTORY

Before we move on to serious hunting strategy, let's take a closer look at the animals we're chasing. Elk are members of the deer family—along with white-tailed deer, mule deer, moose, and caribou—and they originated roughly forty million years ago. As part of the order Artiodactyl, which translates to "having an even number of toes," their two main hooves are symmetrical and are accompanied by two smaller hooves called dewclaws, located higher on the foot. Elk also belong to the suborder of ruminants, which means they have multi-chambered stomachs used to progressively break down tough, woody plant fiber.

These former inhabitants of the open plains are herd animals and, therefore, very sociable. Cows and calves are rarely alone except for a few weeks in the spring when cows give birth. Even bulls are usually found in "bachelor groups," except in the fall when they're in rut and competing for females.

Physically, elk are imposing creatures. An average bull stands five feet at the shoulders and stretches eight feet from nose to tail. The average weight of a male is around 700 pounds, but some exceptional individuals hit the scale at half a ton. Females

A mature bull may weigh 700 to 1,000 pounds. (USFWS)

are somewhat smaller, averaging four and a half feet high and six and a half feet long and weighing about 500 pounds.

Reddish brown in spring and summer, an elk's coat turns tan in fall and winter. Its prominent rump patch is lighter, and its neck and legs are darker than the rest of its body.

Only bulls grow antlers, a process triggered by increasing daylight hours in the spring and accompanied by an increase in the male's testosterone levels. Sprouting from two bony platforms on the skull called pedicles, antlers can grow as much as one inch a day and are formed from successive layers of cartilage that eventually mineralizes into bone. During the roughly 115 days of growth, the antler is protected by a covering, called velvet, that the bull rubs off on trees and bushes in August when the antlers harden and the bull is ready for rut.

A two-year-old bull usually grows small, unbranched antlers known as spikes that may be ten to fifteen inches long. By the third year, he may sport a 4x4 rack consisting of four points, or tines, on each side. Elk with these spindly 4x4 or 5x5 antlers are called raghorns. A six-year-old bull may have a 6x6 rack with more mass. The largest antlers are found on elk that are eleven or twelve years old.

Antlers are status symbols. During rut, a large, massive rack shows rival bulls that its owner is strong and healthy. A bull will also use his antlers as weapons against rival bulls that try to take

Velvet covers an elk's antlers as they grow. Bulls begin rubbing it off by August in preparation for the rut.

his harem—the group of cows he has gathered to mate. Cows also look at the size and mass of a bull's antlers in assessing his merits as a possible mate.

Hunters, on the other hand, look at antlers to assess a bull's trophy status. The eye of the beholder always determines whether a bull is or is not a trophy. A 4x4 raghorn may be a fine trophy on the last day of a long hunting season. But if you're looking for a bull that might go in the record book of an organization like Boone & Crockett, you'll want to look for antlers with a lot of mass, a beam length of about four feet, six or seven points on a side, and a fourth point that is eighteen to twenty inches. Obviously, you can't measure points from afar, but if you see a bull that approaches a trophy class, you'll probably know it. And the more bulls you look at the better your judgment usually becomes.

Antler points don't indicate a bull's age. His teeth do that. Biologists can examine the annual growth rings on a male or female elk's molars to determine how old it is, much like counting the growth rings on a tree. The relative wear on the molars is another way to determine approximate age. Molars become more sloped, rounded, and worn down over years of chewing woody vegetation.

Hunters are usually interested in just two teeth, one on either side of the upper jaw—the canines. Elk canines, also called buglers, ivories, or tusks, have long been highly regarded by Native Indians as decorative adornments for clothing. Elk-tooth dresses, vests, and pendants are often prominent in early photos of Indians. Teeth were also used in trade. In the Rocky Mountains in 1805, the Flathead Indians might have traded a good horse for seventy to eighty ivories. Modern hunters continue to value elk buglers, extracting them from both males and females.

The word "bugler" may come from the fact that bull elk often reveal their canine teeth when they bugle—a vocalization

Antler mass, the number of tines, and personal opinion are all elements of trophy judgment. (Jay Cassell)

that combines a high-pitched squeal and a low-pitched roar. Both male and female elk are extremely vocal. And the bugle is the keystone of a bull's vocabulary. He uses it to advertise his sexual prowess during the mating season, or rut, and we'll discuss this at length in a later chapter. But cows and calves also bark, squeal, mew, grunt, and hiss to communicate alarm, surprise, distress, reassurance, and threat. These vocalizations can be good indicators to hunters that elk are nearby, even though the animals themselves may not be visible.

Elk also communicate with one another through their postures. Both cows and bulls show alarm when they hold their necks high, cock their ears forward, and walk with stiff legs. A submissive elk, on the other hand, holds its head low, drops its ears, and seems to slouch. An elk with its head erect, its ears back, and a front foot raised is signaling its intent to rear on its hind legs and attack with its front feet. Harem-guarding bulls lower their heads level with their backs and hold their antlers back along their flanks. But bulls circling one another in a dominance fight hold their antlers high and tilted toward one another while avoiding eye contact. During rut and throughout the year, hunters can learn a great deal about elk by observing their body language and using it as an intuitive indicator of their intentions.

Rut, of course, marks the time of conception for elk. It usually takes place in early fall, coinciding nicely with many archery seasons throughout the West. After an eight-and-a-half-month gestation period, the calf is born in the spring and stays with the cow through the summer, while bulls are off in small bachelor groups by themselves. During the first winter, both male and female calves remain with their mothers. Young males are the first

When an elk stands stiff-legged with neck erect and ears forward, it's communicating alarm.

to leave during their second year, but young females may stay with their mothers until they give birth to their own calves. Female elk have a life span of around twenty years. Bulls may live about fourteen years—if they don't get shot, of course.

DISTRIBUTION

Hunters tend to think of North American elk as natives of the American West, but natural historians tells us that the true origin is rooted halfway around the world in Asia and Europe, where elk are known as Eurasian red deer. The red deer, it is theorized, slowly immigrated from the Eurasian continent to North America by crossing the Trans-Bering Land Bridge, an isthmus from Siberia to Alaska formed by the lowered water of the Bering Sea during the Illinoian and Wisconsin glacial stages that started about 120,000 years ago and ended roughly 10,000 years ago. Once in Alaska, elk moved down through Canada into much of the United States.

When the Bering Land Bridge was covered by rising sea waters, caused by melting glaciers, the North American elk and the Eurasian red deer were cut off from one another in two distinct populations. Then, in 1758, along came a taxonomist named Linnaeus who classified the Eurasian population as *Cervus elaphus*, commonly called red deer. In 1777 another taxonomist named Erxleben classified the North American population as *Cervus canadensis*, commonly called elk. Naturally, the two classifications suggested that two different species existed.

However, in 1951 a controversy erupted when J. R. Ellerman and T. C. S. Morrison-Scott, in their *Checklist of Palaearctic and Indian Mammals*, listed Eurasian red deer and North American elk as one and the same species. Soon, taxonomic sides were taken. Those in favor of a single species argued that elk and red deer had only been separated for a mere 10,000 years and that they could interbreed and produce fertile offspring, typical of a single species. But those in favor of two separate species claimed that elk were bigger, heavier, and colored differently than red deer and that the complete separation of their natural ranges argued against a single species.

The hoopla was largely put to rest with the 1982 publication of *Elk of North America: Ecology and Management,* in which the conclusion was drawn that: "The existing evidence is in favor of considering the Eurasian red deer and the North American elk as a single species. Since the specific name *elaphus* (Linnaeus 1758) has priority over *canadensis* (Erxleben 1777), the North American elk will be accepted as *Cervus elaphus.*"

End of argument. Maybe.

While North American elk and Eurasian red deer are now considered by most taxonomists, biologists, and natural historians to be of the same species, North American elk have been divided into six subspecies, four of which still survive. Assumed extinct, Eastern elk once roamed much of the inland eastern U.S. from roughly Kansas City, Missouri, to the Atlantic coast (excluding New England and Florida). The extinct Merriam elk inhabited the mountainous terrain of Arizona, New Mexico, Texas, and northern Mexico.

Now numbering less than a thousand, Tule elk live in semi-desert habitat in pockets of California. Manitoban elk, once inhabitants of the Great Plains as far south as the Texas border, now only exist in numbers probably below 10,000 in the Canadian provinces of Manitoba and Saskatchewan.

The Roosevelt elk remains the elk of the Northwest, occupying Afognak Island in Alaska and the western parts of northern California, Oregon, Washington, and British Columbia.

Most numerous of the subspecies, Rocky Mountain elk live in states on either side of the Continental Divide. And small

Tule elk are only found in California, which also has Roosevelt and Rocky Mountain elk. (USFWS)

translocated populations exist in limited areas of the midwestern and eastern U.S. Although Rocky Mountain elk have a somewhat smaller body size than Roosevelt elk, they tend to have longer and wider antlers, making them the most hunted subspecies of North American elk today.

Unfortunately, all North American elk were hunted much too aggressively during the last half of the nineteenth century. By the early 1900s, only 100,000 were thought to survive. By comparison, it's estimated that ten million elk may have roamed the continent before Europeans arrived.

Fortunately, wildlife management has brought elk populations back to an estimated 750,000 today. Elk shipped from Yellowstone National Park (established 1892) and from Wyoming's National Elk Refuge (established 1912) were used to introduce and reintroduce elk populations in many states across the country. Between 1912 and 1967, over 13,500 elk were shipped from Yellowstone National Park to areas in the U.S., Canada, and Mexico.

In the first half of the twentieth century, elk from the Greater Yellowstone Area were used to bolster stocks decimated by hunting or to introduce elk to new areas.

Today, elk inhabit parts of Alaska, Arizona, Arkansas, California, Colorado, Idaho, Kansas, Kentucky, Michigan, Minnesota, Montana, Nebraska, Nevada, New Mexico, North Dakota, Oklahoma, Oregon, Pennsylvania, South Dakota, Texas, Utah, Washington, Wisconsin, and Wyoming. In 2004 there was an elk-hunting season in every one of those states except Texas and Wisconsin. Some states with small elk populations offer very few elk permits to resident hunters only. In other states, like Montana and Colorado in recent years, elk numbers have exceeded management objectives in certain areas. This has increased hunting opportunities for resident and nonresident hunters in the form of expanded seasons and more either-sex hunting.

Washington and Oregon offer hunting for both Roosevelt and Rocky Mountain elk, but only in California can you hunt

▭ Rocky Mountain Elk

▭ Roosevelt Elk

▭ Tule Elk

▭ Manitoban Elk

Roosevelt, Rocky Mountain, and Tule elk—all subspecies of North American elk, or Eurasian red deer, once removed.

If you don't necessarily care about shooting a trophy, Colorado is currently the top state for hunting elk. In 2004, the population was roughly 300,000, and hunters harvested a record 61,174 elk in the state in 2002. Montana is second on the list with 22,447 elk harvested in 2002, and the state harbors some huge bulls in the Missouri River Breaks. Wyoming was close behind, with 21,462 elk killed. Oregon typically has more elk than any states except Colorado and Montana, with a population of roughly 120,000 animals, but their 2002 harvest was 18,368. Idaho has a similar population, although their harvest is usually a bit further behind.

Hunters specifically interested in trophies should look at the White Mountains of Arizona and the Big Horn Mountains of Wyoming as the recent hotspots. And don't overlook Washington, a state that harvested a modest 8,116 in 2002, but also one that produces some fine big-antlered elk.

Chapter 2

WHERE THE ELK ARE

E lk hunters where I live in Montana have a tendency to hang out in cafes until the last week of the season. It's not that they eat more than anybody else; it's just that a western cafe always seems to have a sympathetic ear into which we can grumble about elk and how contrary they are.

Instead of admitting that elk used to be easy to hunt until we drove them from the prairies into the mountains, we bemoan the fact that elk always want to be where we don't want to be. We rail on like this until the snow comes in big dumps to rout the elk from their mountain retreats and bring them down to where we can get at them easily. If it doesn't snow heavily enough, we sit in the cafes *all* season, blaming our unfilled elk tags on the weather and the negative attitude of the beast.

Perhaps that's why Montana's statewide elk hunter success rate averaged 19.67 percent from 1999 to 2002.

At least we're right about one thing: elk want to be where we *don't* want to be. Before the weather forces them onto winter ranges, they hang out on steep slopes at high elevations. They avoid roads, and they look for cover in which it's difficult to see, particularly old stands of timber filled with branches and deadfalls.

Most hunters prefer to wait until heavy snow brings elk down to lower elevations, but that's not always the best way to find animals.

Studies by researchers in Montana's Department of Fish, Wildlife & Parks have confirmed elk preference for these locations during the hunting season.

The elk like these spots because they offer the best security available in their habitat. We don't like these places because they're just plain hard to hunt. Yet this is the terrain we have to hunt if we don't want to wait for the big snow that may never come.

Steep slopes *are* difficult to hunt. They make your legs ache; and sidehill hiking is hard on your ankles, not to mention your lungs. When it's wet or snowy, the slipping and sliding you do makes for twice as much work.

But the same steep slopes that we curse over give the elk a sense of safety. Because these slopes are difficult for predators, especially hunters, to negotiate, elk feel more secure when the ground has a good pitch to it. This terrain provides a more direct exposure to the sun, so steep south- and west-facing slopes hold less snow than flatter areas, making it easier for the elk to move about and find food.

Elk hunters, on the other hand, prefer to stay on main ridgelines and make occasional short forays down those steep side slopes. I had this in mind several years ago when a friend and I decided to hunt up a side ridge in hopes of avoiding other hunters and also finding elk. Within minutes we were winded and had to rest, agreeing that a still-hunter's pace was the only way we could climb the slope and still hope to be steady enough to shoot at an elk if one should appear.

An hour later and only two-thirds of the way to the divide, Chan hunkered behind a tree and motioned for me to stop. He pointed upslope, spreading all five fingers of his hand just above his head. I couldn't see a thing, so I gave him an after-you-Alphonse gesture.

After Chan fired, the thumping of hooves and the cracking of twigs told me we probably wouldn't have to spend the day hauling heavy loads down steep slopes. We spent the next half hour searching for indications of an injured elk. There were none.

While Chan kept shaking his head, I kept saying how the climb had been worth it; we had gotten into elk.

Hunting up steep slopes is not my normal practice. It puts you in a position where elk can easily spot you because they typically bed facing downhill. Rising air currents also can carry your scent to the nostrils of elk that would really rather be left alone. However, I must admit to killing several elk while hunting slowly up steep slopes—and I emphasize the slowly and the steep.

Downhill hunting is preferable, however. It allows you to come on elk from behind, and it keeps your scent above them. Elk seem to stay on the upper half of slopes except in drainage heads, where they tend to use the lower third of the grassy bowls common to those areas.

Of course, steep slopes are just the start of the tough going. Those high elevations don't help either. The higher you go, the longer it takes to get there, the more winded you become, and the farther you are from hot apple pie and coffee. It also gets colder and windier.

It is because hunters resist going to these heights that elk seek them out. Before a heavy snowfall covers the slopes, you can count on a substantial number of elk being at 7,500 to 8,500 feet, which is where I hunt in southwestern Montana. However, this may vary somewhat across the northern Rockies.

It was during the second week in September that I once came upon fifty to sixty elk just below the 9,000-foot divide I was hiking. With fishing rod in hand, I watched two big bulls for over an hour. The bow season had opened the weekend before, and there I was on a fishing trip! It would have taken most of the day to get back down to the trailhead, retrieve my bow, and return. So I pulled my parka hood around my head and just watched elk move in and out of the trees at the edge of an alpine meadow.

Hunting elk at high elevations isn't easy, which is one reason why bulls like to stay up high.

I have also spent my share of days slogging from 5,500 feet to 7,500 feet and then trudging back down again on the same day. I've found elk that way too, but locating them and having enough time to hunt them are different matters. The answer, I'm convinced, is to set up camp. If you can't afford an outfitter, do it yourself. Otherwise, you'll spend most of your time getting to and from your hunting grounds.

It isn't necessary to launch off into the wilderness, nor is it advisable, especially if you're not familiar with the country. But you can get a good topographic map of the area you plan to hunt and locate roads that will get you up to suitable locations. These will probably be logging roads that you can follow to the end and then set up a camp. It may not be the most scenic spot you've ever found, but it will enable you to camp within reasonable striking distance of good elk habitat.

I can't say you'll be *in* habitat, because true to their contrary nature, elk avoid roads. The more traffic a road gets the farther away elk are likely to be, perhaps as far as several miles. But more often elk will keep a good half mile between themselves and the noise and activity associated with roads.

And, yes, we all know a story about a guy who steps out of his truck and pops a big bull. Not too many years ago, friend and neighbor Bart Yeager was driving back from trying to find a moose along Spanish Creek when a lone spike elk showed up in an open meadow near the road. Bart was several miles back down the hill from a jumping-off point for numerous outfitters, so the road got considerable traffic. But there was no denying the existence of that elk, nor the ease with which it became steaks, chops, and burgers.

Yet for most of us this sort of thing is a once in a lifetime occurrence—if it happens at all. Rest assured, if you cruised roads, even old logging roads, as a regular hunting tactic, you'd be sitting on calluses and stepping on your beard before you ever found an elk.

If you want to put elk on the ground consistently, you'll have to do more than just cruise logging roads in your pickup. (Jay Cassell)

So it's necessary to get high, get away from the roads, and find the steep slopes. But even when we do this, most of us want to be able to see considerable distances. Elk prefer not to see very far. They like the thick timber and broken terrain. When they're in places where they can see only short distances, *you* can't see them until you're almost on top of them. In these close quarters, chances are good that elk will scent or hear you before you see them. Limited visibility is clearly to their advantage.

There is a spot in central Montana that—like the rest of the mountain country in the northern Rockies—has been sculptured by past glacial action. This particular area was the site of a terminal moraine where the end of a glacier piled up successive mounds of glacial debris in a series of advances and retreats. The result, as it appears today, is an extensive area of closely spaced hills interspersed with secluded hollows. Standing on the top of any given hill, you can only see into the hollow immediately below. Elk love to hole up in these spots.

Although steep, broken terrain already limits the distance you can see, elk like to throw in an additional security measure. They love to get tucked away in old stands of timber that are also on steep terrain. Those 250- to 300-year-old stands of subalpine fir, Douglas fir, and whitebark pine are perfect. These are places that have never seen a chain saw, so they're dense with trunks and branches.

This is the kind of timber every elk hunter dreads. The thick forest canopy casts shadows that seem to hide an elk near every trunk. Low-hanging branches poke at your eyes, snatch at your hat, and snap at the slightest touch. Deadfalls sprawl thick and slippery, too high to step over and too low to crawl under quietly. And the elk think it's great.

There are two ways to approach these jungles. The first way is to avoid them. Locate the old stands of timber and then figure out where the elk are likely to feed. They aren't going to find much to eat under the cover of thick timber, but that's where they're going to stay during the day when they're pressured. They'll feed out in the open at night and then head back into the timber at first light. If you can locate likely feeding areas that offer good grasses, you can stand hunt early in the morning and late in the evening between the feeding grounds and the thick timber they use as security cover. It's possible that the elk will make their move too early or too late for hunting hours, but you may still be able to spot them and discover where they're using the timber.

This is where the second tactic comes in. There are times when you simply can't avoid going into the timber. But do it only when you have good reason to believe elk are there. Since the way to hunt this thick stuff is by still-hunting—that ever-so-slow, fluid movement through the trees—you'll cover extremely limited

Heading into thick timber after elk takes patience and solid still-hunting skills.

ground. Despite the limited sight range and the numerous noisy obstacles, working heavy cover can pay off.

Under a cairn on a ridge not far from where I sometimes hunt in Idaho there is an iron stake with a brass cap telling anyone who cares to look that the elevation is 7,713 feet. Next to the marker stands an old fir that was hit by lightning. Splinters of its twisted trunk splay out like quills on the back of a riled porcupine. Below the shattered tree and iron stake, a narrow meadow spreads along the ridge for a quarter of a mile. Steep ridges slope off from the meadow's edges to the east and west of the divide. The western slopes are a mosaic of sparse timber and open meadows. To the east the terrain plunges into the dense cover of never-cut fir. The nearest road is down in the bottom of the east drainage, out of sight and sound a good mile and a half away.

It was in this high, ridgetop meadow that I jumped a bull early one morning. I still have an image of the six-point rack disappearing over the rise as hooves sent rooster tails of twigs and snow into the field of my rifle scope. I never got the safety off.

Following the tracks in the shallow snow, I found that the bull had headed downhill into the dense timber on the steep eastern slopes. It seemed useless to follow at the time because I'd stirred things up pretty well. But I came back a few days later. The snow had melted, but fresh droppings indicated that elk had been using the meadow farther down the ridge to the south.

A careful check of my topographic map showed the terrain to the southeast sloping off at a fairly steep yet huntable angle. To the northeast the contour lines crowded closer and closer together to form two distinct ridges dense with timber.

It took me two hours to work down through the old stand of fir on the nearest northeast ridges and another half hour to backtrack and skirt along the divide to the second ridge. Another hour of still-hunting brought me to a miserable tangle of deadfalls that blocked my progress. As I was visually picking a route through the trunks of downed trees and protruding limbs, a graceful bunch of branches on the far side of the maze made a slight but unmistakable turn to the left. At the base of what I'd taken for branches an ear twitched, and then the rest of the bedded bull began to take shape. From what I could figure, I was roughly three-quarters of a mile from the road at the bottom of the drainage. The fallen timber would make it a tough haul out, but it was all downhill. Oh, was it downhill.

Perhaps the most important thing about the bull's selection of that place for security was the fact that it combined all the ingredients of the kind of terrain elk like to hide in and elk hunters hate to hunt. The bull was on a steep slope at a relatively high elevation removed from roads, and he was in old-stand timber where visibility was limited. The combination of all those ingredients is the key to finding elk before the snow socks in.

It required a lot of work to locate that six-point, but sitting in a cafe waiting for winter has never put steaks on the table.

Chapter 3

SIDE RIDGES

If you hunt the Rocky Mountain elk country for thirty years as I have, you will walk a lot. A whole lot. The only thing you'll do as much as walk is ask yourself the following question: Where is the most likely place to find elk? After walking uphill, downhill, and sidehill for so long, I believe I know. Discovering their hiding place was no picnic, and like other great revelations, the truth did not become apparent all at once.

The first time it happened, I didn't think much about *where* it happened. It was early in the season. There was no snow on the ground, and I'd decided I'd better stick to a little-used trail that followed the backbone of a main ridge I liked to hunt. I figured I'd be able to move quietly on the trail, and I did hunt quietly almost all day. I trudged along the ridge for miles; then down one long gulch and up another to the paralleling ridge across the valley; then down that ridge for more miles.

The afternoon had stretched on toward dusk when I started down a side ridge that would lead me to the gravel road. I was moving at a good clip, more intent on beating darkness than on hunting, when a wheezing grunt exploded from a tangle of dead pine not more than twenty yards off the trail. The bull seemed to float noiselessly over the downfalls, as I fell all over myself trying to shoot.

I was still having stern words with myself when I got home. I made a mental note of the thick downfall the elk had been bedded in, but I didn't think much of where the downfall had been located.

The following year a very unlikely event occurred. My neighbor, Norm Strung, was hunting with Dave Petzal one morning after a heavy snow had fallen. Hiking along the top of a divide, they'd found new elk tracks that headed down the nose of a side ridge. The tracks led to a six-point rack not more than fifty yards below the main ridge.

Norm gave Dave the first shot, and as the elk's head went down, another identical head appeared in its place. Norm took his turn. What at first had appeared to be one elk turned out to be two identical six-point bulls bedded down next to one another. Both ended up in the freezer.

I guess it was the storybook nature of the event that kept me from thinking much about where it had occurred. But when Norm pointed out the spot later in the season, I was struck by its similarity to the place I'd jumped my bull the year before. I attributed the likeness, however, to the presence of thick cover in both locations.

Yet another year would pass before I started to put all the pieces together. I'd been hunting the top part of a forested bowl and had come to its far edge, which was formed by a steep side ridge coming off the main divide. It was a ridge that I'd often looked at from above but had never hunted because it seemed so steep.

Before I ever saw the elk, I began to sense he should be there. Walking onto the ridge and peering down the other side, I could

Thick cover on side ridges sometimes holds bulls looking for solitude. (Jay Cassell)

see the forest character change considerably. There were more trees and numerous downfalls, and despite the apparent steepness of the terrain, small secluded terraces shelved out below me. Then, for a moment, I could see him—a big bull moving behind a picket fence of pines on the second terrace. He was gone before I had a chance to raise my rifle.

So there was the two-in-one elk incident of the previous year, the spooked bull of the year before that, and now this. They all happened in thick timber, to be sure, but each time that timber was located on a secluded side ridge. And over the following weeks of haunting innumerable side ridges, I pieced together what I've come to believe are some valid reasons why you're likely to find elk on the side.

Perhaps most important is the fact that side ridges are off the beaten track. They simply don't get the hunting pressure that main ridges do. Main ridges lead somewhere; you can hunt them all day. Side ridges peter out; they're usually steep, and once you go down them you have to climb up again. So side ridges are often left alone by hunters. Preferring not to tangle with hunters, elk find these side ridges to be excellent sanctuaries.

In addition to offering respite from most hunters, these fingers of land can provide good cover. A north-facing side ridge in typical elk habitat is heavy in forest growth. Frequently, it has extensive areas of brush and blowdowns that are ideal escape zones. And even though an entire ridge may not have suitable escape cover, one side may be thickly timbered.

The vantage points offered to an elk on a side ridge are also important. From his bed he can look down on most of the country below, and he can depend on the daytime upslope breezes to carry any foreign scents to his sensitive nostrils. Finally, most side ridges are close to food. Where there's northern exposure, a southern exposure can't be far away. Southern exposures in the West usually mean places where wild grasses grow. These grasses are the elk's favored food. An elk can find cover on a northern side ridge during the day, then pop over the main ridge to a southern exposure for feeding in the morning and evening.

Elk prefer to bed down in areas where they can see the country below and escape quickly from predators.

This was in my head one morning while I was on my way to a side ridge that I was sure would hold elk. Six to eight inches of snow had fallen the day before and through the night, but the sky was clearing as I approached a high point on the main divide where a meadow led down to the start of the ridge.

Because an open park was not a place I expected to find an elk, especially during daylight hours, I wasn't prepared for the bull that fled across the meadow as I topped the divide. His departing hooves raised clouds of fine snow, and they raised questions in my own mind. I had satisfied myself on the "whys" of side-ridge elk, but there appeared to be some questions of "when" and even "where" to clear up before I could refine my hunting tactics.

My basic thinking had been sound. Elk *are* most likely to be found on side ridges during daylight hours, except in the early morning and late afternoon when they may be feeding or moving to and from feeding grounds. However, after a prolonged storm—during which elk tend to seek cover—they may feed out in the open well into the day. That was a fine point I'd overlooked on this particular morning.

I've discovered some other fine points during my years of in-the-trees training. A bull will almost always bed down on the top half of a side ridge, and invariably he'll be facing downhill. I suspect this offers elk the optimum position for surveying the surroundings while chewing their cuds and resting. Still, it's unlikely that you'll ever come across an elk sleeping during the day.

Elk also seem to prefer side ridges that are broken by terraces. These shelves may only be the size of a small room or they may cover several acres, but they offer some level bedding ground in terrain that is often fairly steep.

Discovering the answers to some of the "whens" and "wheres" of side-ridge elk has helped me work out specific approaches to hunting elk in mountainous country. When there is no snow on the ground for tracking purposes, I confine my elk hunting to heavily timbered side ridges with access to grasses. The higher in elevation and the more remote these ridges, the better, because the absence of snow is a good indication that the elk have not gotten nature's signal to move from their summering grounds along the high divides down to lower elevations.

Once snow has arrived, check out the main ridges first to see if there are any tracks crossing from one side to the other or coming down and leading off to a specific side ridge. A main ridge can easily have a dozen or more side ridges, and the more you narrow the possibilities, the better your chances of finding an elk. If no tracks appear along a main ridge, I start checking out the side ridges that provide the most secure elk habitat. Although a

Tracks in the snow will often lead you from a main ridgeline to a side-ridge pocket where elk take refuge during daylight hours.

main ridgeline offers the easiest access to a side ridge, elk sometimes take a route that's parallel to, but below, the ridge. The tracks may run only 100 feet from where you walk, but if you can't see them, they're as good as nonexistent.

Because a bedded elk will probably be looking downhill and because the air currents are likely to be rising from below, you should try to approach side ridges from above. In order to come down the ridges with the best elk habitat, you can get into the high country via draws and gulches and on ridges that are fairly open.

Hunting downhill also gives you the advantage of being less winded than when hunting uphill. A number of years ago, before I'd smoothed out my approaches to hunting elk on the side, I was working up a steep side ridge through heavy snow. Even moving slowly, I couldn't help getting winded. When I saw the bull, he was already eyeballing me from his bed. It was a split-second stare of discovery that told me there was no time to catch my breath, and then the elk erupted into motion. My huffs continued rhythmically over the ringing of the shot in my ears, and the elk was swallowed by the timber without so much as a part in his hair.

Even when you're hunting down a ridge, you should move very slowly, not only to keep from getting winded but to keep from spooking elk. Since thick timber is an integral element in the side-ridge habitat, you'll have to get close to an elk before you'll be able to see it. But you won't be able to get close to it unless you move slowly and quietly.

It was toward the end of the first season after I'd discovered the phenomenon of side-ridge elk that I was finally able to put some of my new tactics to use. While hiking up an open side draw to get onto a main ridge of Montana's Gallatin Range, I crossed what seemed to be fresh elk tracks in a patch of soft dirt. The tracks indicated the direction the elk had headed, but they soon disappeared in the grass, and I was unable to find them again. I suspected the elk had recently been feeding on the grass and with the coming of daylight had left to find cover. I knew the ridge on the other side of the divide was thick in timber, and since the tracks pointed that way it seemed a likely spot to check out.

In an hour and a half, I hadn't traveled more than three-quarters of a mile. but I had no choice; the dry conditions dictated that pace. To have gone faster would have meant good-bye to any elk that might have been in the neighborhood. Nevertheless, I was beginning to get discouraged as I approached the bottom half of the ridge.

As soon as the twig snapped beneath my boot, the elk was on his feet, and I eased down on one knee. The bull was wary, but my scent had not reached him. He moved slowly in back of the lodgepole, his four points no trophy but ample confirmation of my hunting theories. As the elk's shoulders moved into the frame of two trees, I squeezed off the shot.

KNUCKLE-CRACKING ELK

An elk is an animal of both open and forested country, so it needs two different ways of warning other elk of danger, ways that are appropriate to the different habitats. In open terrain, elk tend to be noisy—grunting, squealing, and barking communications with their neighbors as they feed and rest. They show no concern that their noisiness will alert predators to their whereabouts, because they can see any predators that may attempt to get near them.

It is the sudden absence of elk noise in open country that alerts other elk to danger. When neighboring elk abruptly fall silent, it's time to look around and take notice. This silence, followed by a rigid stance and then a high-stepping, halting gait (called a "warning gait") is the open country signal of alarm.

In forested or brushy terrain, elk have been conditioned to keep quiet, with the exception of bulls in rut. The noisy behavior that they exhibit in open terrain could be dangerous where visibility is limited, allowing predators to sneak up unheard by "chatty" elk. Just the act of feeding and moving about makes some noise. But elk have a unique way of distinguishing the sounds of their own movement from that of predators. Like caribou, elk leg joints give off an audible click similar to knuckle cracking when they take a step. These clicks, which nearby elk are aware of as they feed or rest, tick off the rhythm of their walking movements. So when the general pattern of knuckle cracking suddenly stops in areas where elk are surrounded by vegetation, it's the sound of alarm. Elk look up to check out their companions. If their neighbors display the warning stance and the warning gait cause for alarm is real, and all elk in the vicinity take off through the trees.

Chapter 4

ON THE STEEP

When a six-point bull erupts from behind a crumpled escarp-
ment while you're balancing on the points of rocks to cross
a talus slope, it may occur to you that elk have something in common with mountain goats: They equate steepness with security.

True, when we ponder elk in hiding, most of us look to timber, pole stands, deadfalls, and brush. But a steep slope may be
an elk's hideout of choice during the hunting season. Pushed by
humans from the plains, through the hills, into the mountains,
elk may be conditioned to know that there will be fewer hunters
on steeper slopes. Yet elk on the steep gain more than a sense of
security. They're provided with everything else necessary to live
in relative comfort—day in, day out—for the entire length of the
hunting season.

Their sense of security is backed by a first-class escape
clause, if the need arises. Elk turn steep terrain to their advantage come flight time. Sprinting downhill, they can put hundreds of yards between themselves and danger by letting gravity
do most of the work. Only after they gain a comfortable distance do they angle into a traverse of the terrain and finally into
a slower uphill climb. But even when powering up a steep

Elk love the security provided by steep slopes.

snow-covered pitch, an elk's legs are more than a match for the most fanatic pursuer.

Steepness, when combined with proper aspect, also equals shallower snow cover. South-facing slopes are the first to lose snow because of the more direct angle of the sun, and because there is less shade and more exposure to wind. This gives elk greater mobility and more access to forage, grass and low shrubs that may be flattened beneath deep snow elsewhere on their range. Bedding sites flat enough to keep an elk from tumbling off a hill are usually available on the steep in the form of occasional terraces and niches behind uprooted trees and rock outcroppings. So elk can be happy for the whole hunting season camped out up there where we prefer not to go.

Elk use slopes up to 40 percent as readily as they'd flip up their heels on the sprawling and gentle plains. But thankfully for serious hunters, they don't much care for steep terrain once the angle of the countryside tips much over 50 percent. (Keep in mind that large avalanches can occur on slopes of only 25 percent, although they are most common on slopes between 60 and 100 percent, which translates to 30 to 45 degrees.)

Elk tend to float toward the top third of the slope. These upper reaches have definite advantages. They provide plenty of plunge room for quick escape. And the top of a slope offers easy access to the benefits of both southern and northern aspects—south during the day for warmth and forage, north at night for the thermal containment of forest cover, which is usually thicker on that side.

The steeps most likely frequented by elk during the hunting season are removed from the typically tramped trails that

Hunters who pursue elk on the steep must be in good shape.

hunters follow along main divides. Elk take up residence on side or spur ridges that sneak unobtrusively off major backbones of the topography. This doesn't mean these slopes are hidden in remote and wild country. They are probably a part of the terrain you already hunt.

As a dividend for spending the energy to reach these high-angled haunts, you'll discover that the elk most likely to seek the security of the steep are the bulls. And that may be enough to motivate most elk hunters up the steepest of hills.

Chapter 5

THICK TIMBER

A ll of us who hunt elk have a recurring dream of coming upon a large herd grazing calmly in an open meadow where we can survey the possibilities and select the perfect bull for our wall and freezer. But it's a dream that quickly turns to nightmare when we actually face the reality of hunting elk on a large portion of their range. Although there are some areas on the east slopes of the Continental Divide where extensive natural openings do exist, most of the good elk habitat on the west side of the Rocky Mountains is forested. In order to hunt elk in these spots, you have no choice but to go into the woods after them.

The general forest elevation at which you can expect to find elk during the hunting season depends on the weather. Early in the season, before really cold and snowy conditions hit the high country, elk may be distributed from foothills to alpine bowls, with most at higher elevations. Once a good taste of winter comes to these higher haunts, however, elk move down to mid elevations where weather conditions are not as severe. As winter sets in here, they descend even farther to occupy the forest just above open winter range in the foothills.

Within these general elevation zones, elk move to the areas of the forest that get the least hunting pressure. They avoid going near roads—even logging roads—that get frequent use, and they tend to move into thick timber during the day and come into spaced timber at night. There's no doubt that the pressure of hunting season forces elk to use their home habitats differently than they would if they were left undisturbed. This is made laughingly clear to me year after year when the elk where I live reappear on sunny, open hillsides within days of the close of hunting season.

The places elk seek within the forest fulfill specific needs at specific times. During hunting season, hiding and escape cover are prime concerns that are related primarily to how far they (and you) can see through the trees. During the day, elk look for forest cover that provides relatively little sight distance. As I touched on earlier, the elk's reasoning seems to be that if they can't see very far through the trees, neither can you. Also, chances are pretty good that under these conditions they're going to hear or smell you before you see them.

Forest cover is a matter of tree trunk or branch density, and it can be found in several situations. Lodgepole thickets where pines from four to six inches in diameter grow close together are called "dog hair" pine in my neck of the woods, and elk love to move into the middle of these dense stands when they get nervous. Although each individual tree offers little cover, collectively they put up quite a screen.

Older forest stands don't have trees growing so close together, but they do have more massive trunks that limit how far you can see. These older stands also have a fair amount of deadfalls that block sight distance and slow any would-be pursuers. I have a very clear image from years ago of ducking under a fallen tree and seeing, from my crouched position, numerous elk rear-

Areas with mixed tree cover provide elk refuge after feeding. Unfortunately for hunters, these places are difficult to reach undetected.

ends bobbing easily over a maze of downed trees. You can bet that I wasn't about to follow their route of departure.

Perhaps the ideal hiding place for elk is a forest with two or more layers. For example, an older stand of lodgepole pine, whose branches are all at the top, often has an understory of sub-alpine fir with branches that go all the way to the ground. Elk love to get into a spot like this when they're feeling pressured. In fact, studies suggest that the most preferred elk bedding sites are found in timber that has 75 to 100 percent tree-crown cover.

In most cases, this kind of thick forest cover, whether in the form of young, dense stands or older, multi-layered stands, is going to be found on north or east slopes where moisture encourages heavier forest growth. These are the slopes to hunt, especially in the middle of the day.

Look for relatively level, timbered terraces on otherwise steep hillsides or ridges. These are excellent pockets on which to pinpoint your midday hunting activities.

But elk have to eat, and thick forest cover doesn't offer much in the way of grasses, herbs, and forbs that elk hunger for. It's the sparse forest cover that provides good groceries for these ungulates in the fall. You won't find elk feeding in areas where crown density is much more than about 25 percent.

Partial forest cover over feeding grounds is desirable, however. By fall, grass in open meadows has been pretty well dried up by the sun or zapped by frost. But under the partial cover of trees, grass gets enough sun to grow without burning up, and it also gets some protection from light frosts. This sparser forest growth is more often found on south- and west-facing slopes where elk usually move to feed at night during hunting season.

So when elk are being hunted they seek out a place with a balance of thick and sparse forest cover. The closer these hiding and feeding sites are to each other, the better the elk like them because relatively little movement is required to satisfy their basic needs. This is one reason elk tend to occupy the upper slopes of ridges and divides. The thick escape timber on the top of a north or east slope can be easily reached from the top of a south or west feeding ground simply by popping over the ridge. In some cases, it may be a matter of traveling only a few hundred yards. When you find one side of a ridge offering cover and the other offering food, you've found an excellent place to hunt elk in timber.

In addition to hiding and escape cover and partially covered feeding grounds, elk often seek thermal cover in the fall. The weather during hunting season can be extremely variable. The temperature might be in the sixties or seventies one week and below zero the next. When it's hot, elk can't take off their winter coats, so they look for a microclimate that will be cooler than the rest of the forest. Conversely, when it's bitter cold and windy, even an elk's coat can't keep it as warm as it would like.

It has been estimated that elk lose twice as much body heat standing on an exposed hill as they do in the shelter of a forest. Also, wind speeds can be cut in half in the shelter of a hollow or draw, and if the draw is heavily timbered the effects of the wind may be reduced by nearly 90 percent. When the weather is windy and cold the best thermal protection for elk is a dense forest canopy with tall crowns combined with understory vegetation. The overstory slows radiant heat loss, and the understory slows the wind. The best chance of finding this combination is in old-growth timber.

There is a spot where I frequently hunt elk that starts as a tight, deep cleavage near the top of a north slope. The locals call it "the Hole." The name is appropriate for a number of reasons.

In cold weather, elk retreat from exposed hillsides to heavy cover that helps them retain body heat.

Near its upper reaches you can walk to the edge and peer down into a tangle of deadfalls and bushes. As the Hole descends, it widens and gradually fills with closely spaced firs. For most of its length it is not an easy place for a man to walk. But on cold, windy days in November I have eased up to the edge of the Hole and seen elk congregated in small, protected groups while I shivered in the bitter wind above them. This is the best kind of forested pocket to hunt when the weather turns nasty.

If the weather isn't miserable, locating elk in timber may require a more systematic approach. Early in the season you may want to try hunting in saddles or along natural trailways between patches of thick timber on one side of a ridge and patches of sparse timber—where the grass is still green and succulent—on the other side. Don't bother with these locations unless there are plenty of indications of elk use: tracks, dug-up turf, and fresh droppings. You'll also have to be there early in the day in order to catch elk before they slip back into the thick timber from their feeding grounds. You might even want to make a cold camp (no fire or stove) the night before so you can be in place at first light without making any disturbance.

By the end of the first week of the season, however, elk in all but the most secluded places are going to be gun-shy. They'll be firmly ensconced in their favorite timbered tangle by daybreak. You'll have no choice but to go in after them.

The only way to hunt timber for elk is to move very slowly and cover your ground thoroughly. Zero in on three or four north- or east-side ridges along a divide, then stalk each ridge, going up one side and down the other. Move so you can look down one side of the ridge while going up and the other side while going down. Don't retrace any ground, and concentrate your hunting on the upper halves of the ridges.

If there is snow on the ground, you may be lucky enough to find fresh elk tracks when you're using this methodical approach to hunting. Although the discovery of new tracks quickens the pulse, don't let it quicken your pace. Anything but an extremely slow stalk through timber is likely to be a giveaway. Elk are in their element in timber. You may have to tip-toe through the trees for hours to successfully come up on an elk that was only half a mile away when you cut its tracks. You never know where that elk is going to go; he may be bedded behind the next up-rooted tree stump or on the terrace directly below you.

With or without snow on the ground, remember this about pursuing elk in timber: it's close hunting. You'll be within 100 yards before you're able to see them, often much, much closer. The only way to get that close without giving yourself away is to creep at a snail's pace. What promising terrain you don't cover today, you can try tomorrow, or the next day, or the day after. That's the elk hunter's refrain when it comes to hunting timber.

Chapter 6

UNDERCOVER ELK

I once saw a cartoon that showed two bull elk sitting in a porta-ble blind made out of bushes and tree branches. The elk had cameras around their necks and were surrounded by hunters. One elk was saying to the other, "This morning I got a great shot of one in full hunter orange."

The cartoon made me laugh because it was so close to the truth. Elk are so adept at using cover you'd think they carried por-table blinds around with them. For animals that once populated the open plains and grass prairies, they've wasted no time in be-coming experts in the art of going undercover.

Although elk seek cover to hide, they also use it as protection from the weather and as a place to find food, as well as avenues for travel. Each of these benefits is found in different kinds of cover and in different areas of an elk's home range. So if you un-derstand the different types of cover and how they provide for an elk's needs, you can make smart decisions on where and how to hunt elk in any location.

PROTECTION FROM WEATHER

When they're seeking relief from temperature extremes, elk are most likely to be found in areas with dense forest canopies. An "umbrella" of trees makes for cooler temperatures during cold weather. This thermal cover usually comes in the form of overstory density that blocks out the sunlight needed for understory growth. As a result, elk may go undercover in an effort to escape from the extremes of heat or cold yet still be quite visible to hunters walking through the forest. So much for the portable blind theory.

This same type of cover is very effective in moderating snow depths. A thick overstory catches snow before it lands on the ground. It also prevents ice crusts, caused by sun and wind, which may be found in open grassland. So elk also seek thick forest canopies when snow conditions in more open terrain make movement and foraging difficult.

Tree canopies often keep snow levels low on the forest floor, making it easier for elk to move and feed. (USFWS)

As a result, one of the very best times to hunt elk occurs just after a heavy snowstorm that is followed by a cold front. The snow effectively muffles the sounds of your ungraceful movements, and the elk congregate in predictable areas of high-density overstory where you can see them thanks to the low-density understory. In extreme cold, individual elk, especially lone bulls, may seek the protection of snow wells that form at the base of isolated trees with thick branches hanging close to the ground. While two or three feet of snow may accumulate around the tree, the ground under the branches is often completely bare.

Years ago, while hunting on snowshoes, I was approaching just this kind of tree when its branches started shaking furiously, setting off an avalanche of snow. Out from the back side of the tree stormed a bull, which very effectively eluded my lone shot. Figuring I'd already scared off every other animal in the vicinity, I took the time to climb beneath the draping branches. I discovered an area so snug and comfortable that I could've set up housekeeping. Since then I've paid close attention to low-slung trees, memorizing their locations on the elk ranges I hunt frequently. More than once I've jumped elk out of cozy holes beneath these trees.

Snow wells offer cover from the wind as well as the cold, but elk more often look to topography and low vegetation for wind protection. The lee side of a ridge, a narrow draw, and a hollow between surrounding hills are all worth checking out when the wind is howling through the trees. When elk move into thick brush or downfalls to find wind cover, however, you're better off waiting outside. Your chances of moving into such a place undetected are about as good as winning a foot race with a cheetah.

A PLACE TO FIND FOOD

We tend to think of elk as open-land feeders, grass-eaters that fill their bellies at night when we can't hunt them. But things begin to happen in the fall that may actually shift favored feeding locations into the cover of timber.

Elk love grass. They especially love early growth grass because it's tender and succulent and loaded with nutrition. By fall, though, grass that's growing out in the open is usually old and rank or dried out from the sun or nipped by early frosts or covered by early snow. Under sparse forest cover, on the other hand, shaded grass doesn't develop until later in the summer, and it may have just reached its prime by the time elk season rolls around. So elk move into these areas during the fall to find the last of the best grass available before winter closes down around them.

This sparse forest cover, especially when situated in moist areas on western slopes, is a good place to look for elk during moderate weather when hunting pressure isn't too great. Morning and evening are the most likely times to find elk, but I've had success in this kind of cover at midday too, especially in areas where it adjoins thick understory cover that elk can slip in and out of easily.

These feeding spots should be approached from above and at an extremely slow pace. You'll also do well to work down along the border of sparse timber and thicker cover. This is where elk move if spooked. If you're situated between the elk and where they want to go, they may show a certain amount of confusion that can be to your advantage.

Sparse timber accompanied by topographical cover is another excellent place to hunt at any time of day. Secluded draws and hard-to-find pockets or bowls attract elk because they offer some level of visual security. The density of such areas assure elk that since their field of vision is limited, yours must be, as well.

One of the easiest elk hunts I ever had occurred in this combination of sparse timber cover and surrounding topographical

Sparse timber gives elk a place to eat late-season grass.

cover. I'd been working the edge of a steep, west-facing draw, paying more attention to the thick timber on the north side than the
thinner forest on the south. In fact, the thicker trees probably
helped conceal me until a slight movement, and that distinctive
elk color, caught my eye across the draw. Not one but two five-
point bulls stood shoulder to shoulder grazing at 12:30 in the

afternoon. I've stopped telling the part about how I had time to check out each set of antlers before choosing the one I wanted. It never fails to bring boos and raspberries from my friends, who have trouble dealing with the truth at times.

AVENUES FOR TRAVEL

Elk are movers; that's one of the reasons they're difficult to hunt. And although they will move miles out into the open to feed at night, daytime travel is usually restricted to areas where cover is available.

In places where numerous naturally open parklands are interspersed with forest, elk use woodland corridors as travel lanes. In the fall, they may feed along the forest border, not venturing into the open much at all. However, if you know that elk are feeding at night in specific meadows that are surrounded by fingers of forest, take an early morning stand in these travel avenues, particularly where they lead back into thick escape timber where elk can find daytime security.

Another important undercover travel route can often be found in timber located just below open ridges. Elk seem to favor north slopes where the forest is thickest and where they can travel for miles paralleling the ridgeline. They use these routes for moving to lower elevations when big storms hit in the high country. So if you have good timing and some patience you can take a stand near one of these trails and possibly see dozens, sometimes hundreds, of elk walking single file through the trees. I've witnessed this twice; it's a sight that gave me goose bumps.

A much more reliable spot for catching undercover elk on the move is in a timbered saddle during the first few days of the hunting season. Most good elk habitat in the West is typified by a series of drainages descending from the flanks of major mountain ranges. These drainages are divided by ridges that are often steep and high. An elk wanting to get from one drainage to another will look for the easiest route across a ridge. That means a saddle, especially if it has good cover.

Any elk trying to escape heavy hunting pressure in one drainage is going to head for a saddle soon after hunting season starts. Some of the country I hunt includes a popular, easily reached canyon where hunters flock on opening day. Both adjoining canyons have no roads, and though there are a handful of saddles along a ten-mile stretch, they take some huffing and puffing to get into. The day before the season opens, I often camp near one of these saddles. At times I've sat for a day or more at a good vantage point overlooking a timber saddle and thought I made the wrong decision. But I usually see elk—one, two, three days into the season. After that, it's time to look elsewhere, because a day or two of rifle fire and commotion in the woods makes elk dust off their portable blinds.

PLACES TO HIDE

Of all the needs elk have for cover, none is as important as a place to hide, and escape or security cover is the kind that makes hunters curse. When they're serious about not being seen elk try to put something tangible between you and them. Bushes, branches, downfall, tree trunks, rocks, and ridges are all suitable shields. The thicker the shield, the better they like it.

Unlike thermal cover, hiding cover requires understory density. Elk like to hide in old-growth timber that has lots of low branches and tangled deadfalls, or they head for very thick stands of "dog hair" saplings. I've found elk in these closely spaced pole stands, and it has made me a jibbering wreck. Even if you're able to move in on them without notice, you can't tell which antlers belong to which animals or even what body parts belong with each other. The elk can be maddeningly close, but they're safe from any hunter with an ounce of discretion.

Of course, these dense stands of old- and new-growth hiding cover are particularly attractive to elk if they're on steep slopes, and they are rarely found close to roads with even light traffic. When hunting pressure is heavy, these dense, usually remote spots are where elk spend most of the daylight hours.

It is almost impossible to hunt successfully inside good hiding cover. Sometimes you must do some serious scouting to find where elk have been hiding and where they have been feeding, and then post yourself between these areas early in the morning. While it's possible that elk will move back into heavy hiding cover before it's light enough to hunt, this strategy may offer your only opportunity to intercept elk that have gone undercover to avoid hunting pressure.

Clearly, elk use different cover to satisfy different needs. So it stands to reason that the closer together these cover types are to one another the more elk will use them. This diversity of cover usually comes closest together where the terrain faces a number of different directions. Hunting along the upper portions of north-south running divides with east-west facing ridges, for example, can provide optimum opportunities for locating undercover elk at any time of day under any conditions. Elk may be undercover, but at least you have a chance of catching them with their blinds down.

A NOD OF THE HEAD

The longer an elk's antlers grow, the more movement they show at the tips when the elk moves his head. This phenomenon acts as a long-distance indicator to other elk—and to hunters—of the bull's presence and his relative size.

Chapter 7

DOG-HAIR PINE FORESTS

There's nothing like building a fence to bring out your elk-hunting instincts. The year my son started to totter on his own chubby feet, I knew it was time to fence off the creek that runs in front of our house. Armed with a Forest Service permit, I urged my 4x4 up an abandoned logging road to the edge of a pole thicket closely packed with lodgepole pines that measured five to six inches in diameter and reached heights of twenty-five to thirty feet. They were ideal for the posts and poles I needed to keep young Patrick from becoming amphibious.

Working close to the ground, felling trees and cutting them into proper lengths, I was surprised by the amount of old elk droppings that covered the forest floor. It was July, and the dried, crumbly droppings suggested that the elk hadn't been there in months. I could only speculate on when they'd used the spot in such numbers.

Winter seemed like the most logical time. The wind I'd felt in the open meadow before entering the pole patch had been reduced to a light breeze by the understory shrubs and the closely spaced tree trunks with their low limbs, making this a good spot for elk to hole up in during a winter storm. In addition to cutting the wind chill, the trees offered protection from radiant heat loss, thanks to the thick canopy overhead.

Yes, I decided as I hauled my load of poles out of the forest, the elk had probably been there in January when the temperature hit −41 degrees and I was tinkering with frozen pipes and wondering about the long-term effects of living through winters in the northern Rockies.

The following day I was back for another load of materials. My friend George had promised to meet me after lunch to help truck out the last of the poles.

"I could hear your chain saw," he said when he arrived. "But I'll be darned if I could see you until I was about to step on your tail."

"Told you it was a real dog-hair patch of pine," I laughed.

"Dog hair! Heck, an army could hide in here and nobody'd see it."

George has a penchant for things military. He likes to read about the tactics and strategies of armies in action, and his house is full of books about the Civil War and the World Wars. But wars make me sad; they're bad for your health. I'd rather contemplate elk. And if George could picture a whole army taking refuge in the pole patch, I could see an entire elk herd hiding there.

And why not? That pole patch would be a great place for elk to elude hunters during the fall. In many respects it offered more security than the mature and old-growth timber we usually think of as providing both thermal and hiding cover and where I'd spent most of my time looking for elk. The tree trunks certainly weren't very big, but what they lacked in size they made up for in numbers, and their low-hung branches screened elk from sight more effectively than the biggest of trees. By the time I pulled out of that dog-hair growth of timber, I'd decided it would be one of the first places I'd look for elk in the fall.

Lodgepole pine forests are miserable to hunt but sometimes shelter large numbers of elk.

Well, the fence got built, and the summer flew to a conclusion like all summers do in regions of changing seasons. And when elk season opened, I'd forgotten about the pole patch. All I could think about was the inordinate number of hunters that had suddenly materialized and the apparent disappearance of elk in the area I hunted.

For the first four or five days of the season, despite the hunting pressure, the elk came out onto open grassland to feed at night and then headed for the timber during the day. It was a routine I was used to from past seasons. But by the end of the week the elk had stopped feeding in the open—even at night. They were obviously finding their groceries elsewhere.

We tend to think of elk as grass-eaters, and grass certainly is their preference, but elk have an exceptional digestive capacity, and they can get along on a wide variety of foods, including the stems and twigs of woody vegetation. In addition to having the ability to adapt to a variety of foods, elk are explorers. They are constantly checking out new niches in their environment for available food and cover, even if they don't use them at the time of discovery. It's a way of hedging their bets against hard times. And times don't get much harder for elk than the middle of a high-pressure hunting season.

I was thinking just that when the pole patch popped back into my mind. Not only did it provide protection from the weather and offer a good place to hide from hunters, but it also came supplied with food. The slow changes of forest succession had not yet shaded out the understory of edible shrubs. Huckleberry, snowberry, and the occasional wild rose still grew on the forest floor—all woody plants the elk could eat. In fact, they could probably survive in one of those pole patches for weeks, or at least until the end of the hunting season, without having to come out.

Before daylight the next morning, I was easing up to the pole thicket on foot after having left my vehicle a half mile back on the rutted logging road. After an hour of hunting in areas where I'd seen ample signs of elk the previous summer, I'd satisfied myself that the elk weren't there. But, oh, had they been there! Fresh droppings were everywhere, and they weren't more than a day old. I'd missed the elk by a whisker.

Where, I thought, would I find similar patches of pole timber? I knew there was one on the other side of the drainage a few miles away. A forest fire had burned thirty or forty acres there in the 1950s, and in a low light you could tell, even from a distance, that the forest had an entirely different color and texture than the surrounding old-growth timber. Another island of dog-hair pine grew back in Shirley Canyon, where forest regeneration had occurred following a clearcut made decades ago.

Wherever patches of pole occur—whether lodgepole pine in Montana and Wyoming or western hemlock in Idaho—they are a product of forest succession, and they'll occur in areas where past vegetation has been removed by fire, logging, disease, flooding, or windfall. The best patches of poles usually grow on north- and east-facing slopes where moisture and sunlight are most conducive to dense timber growth. I figured I still had time to check the north-slope pole patch up in Shirley Canyon; it was sure to be a fall hideaway for at least some elk.

Now, discovering why elk used pole patches during the hunting season and figuring out where to find those patches was easy compared with the problem of determining the best way to actually hunt elk in dog-hair timber. That problem, of course, is the reason elk choose pole patches for refuge. You can't just wade into a thicket of dog-hair timber and hunt elk. You're too vulnerable. But there are three approaches you can try.

The first is to stay out of the dog hair altogether. This method involves just sitting and waiting. Now, elk hunters—more than any other hunters I know—have the hardest time doing nothing. Whitetail hunters are used to taking a stand, or they're resigned to it or believe it's the only way to get their game. But elk hunters are an antsy lot. We want to be on the move.

Nevertheless, dog-hair elk, especially at first and last light, are best hunted on your duff at the edge of pole timber. When choosing a stand, search the area for any tracks in the snow or soft earth that indicate elk may be entering and exiting the pole patch. Consider the direction the elk would likely head if they were to leave the patch with an appetite for grass. Then take a stand near that spot. If the elk are using the dog hair as a daytime refuge only, morning and evening are the times you'll intercept them. If they're holed up in the timber over the long haul, these are the times when you're most likely to see them up and about.

This passive approach is a game of patience and conviction: the patience to sit it out day after day, and the conviction that all track and sign indications point to elk using that pole patch. Elk may not even be there the first or second or third day you take a stand. But fifty or sixty of them may parade past on the fourth morning of your hunt.

The second approach to hunting dog-hair elk puts you on your feet, and you can use it in the middle of the day. It's a tactic based on the elk's fondness for ecotones, those boundary lines where two different habitat types meet. In areas where pole patches border brushfields or natural openings, there is a wider variety of forage plants available to elk than in the heart of the dog hair. This availability, combined with the animal's own restlessness during the course of a day, often brings elk out to the edge of a dense stand of poles to feed. Here, they can eat well and still have one hoof in escape cover.

One method of hunting dog-hair pines is to take a stand along travel routes to and from such areas. It takes patience, but you never know when a large herd will pass through.

By still-hunting—and I mean moving very slowly—around the edge of a pole thicket, it's possible to catch elk that have been lured to the edge of their cover by hunger. I've found that these border areas are often easier to walk through quietly than either of the habitats which form them.

Of all the approaches to hunting dog-hair timber, none beat getting into the thick of the trees. It isn't always possible, but there are more manmade and natural paths that lead into pole timber than you might expect. Old logging roads sometimes traverse such patches, and hiking trails often cut through them. The elk themselves, through frequent use, tend to make game trails that can be navigated by a careful hunter.

Finding these routes into dog-hair thickets is something that's best done before the season begins. Scouting can be done in the summer when you can locate and follow likely pathways to discover exactly where they'll take you. I've even been known to remove a pesky obstacle here and there to make my hunting season forays as noiseless as possible. It's sort of like trimming a branch or two from above a favorite trout stream. But the most important concern is finding a pathway into the dog hair.

Occasionally, you'll be surprised by what your scouting turns up. The first year I hunted in the West, I spent a considerable amount of time trying to get the lay of the land near my home. On one particular scouting trip, I blundered into some dog-hair timber that just about swallowed me up. I'd thrashed through it for forty-five minutes when the trees abruptly opened up onto a twenty-foot-wide swath that ran like a surveyor's cut through the dog hair. At the time, the fire break, which had been cut by the Forest Service, was simply a miraculous way out of a bushwhacking situation. Since I've discovered the ways of dog-hair elk, however, I've used that grand avenue through dense pole timber for an altogether different purpose.

Chapter 8

WET MEADOWS

Decades of forest suppression in the elk habitat of the West have given rise to the vast expanses of mature and stagnated lodgepole pine forests that often cover 90 percent or more of the elk range. Scattered throughout this dense cover are small wet meadows associated with streams, springs, ponds, and swamps. Although wet meadows often occupy as little as 5 percent of the area, elk may spend as much as half their time grazing and resting in them. This makes such places ideal for elk hunting.

Elk are attracted to wet meadows because of the large amount of food available therein, as compared to the amount found in forests. Very little forage is able to grow under dense canopies of lodgepole, so while elk may use thick forests for travel, resting, and escape, they must look elsewhere for good grazing grounds.

Moist areas in the forest tend to have deep, wet soil that produces prolific growth of plants such as alpine timothy, marsh marigold, western yarrow, water sedges, fleabane, and mountain bluebells. The forbs are the main attraction for elk during the summer in these areas, but the sedges keep them coming back in the

Elk love to eat vegetation that thrives in well-watered areas. (USFWS)

fall. Typically, elk start grazing in wet meadows about half an hour after first light and continue until about 10 AM. Then they rest and ruminate until around 4 PM, when they start to graze again.

While wet meadows provide excellent forage, they are also good places for elk to rest. Openings created by the meadows are rarely wider than fifty feet, so the high trees surrounding them give elk a sense of security. In addition, fallen trees, shrubs, and tall grasses within the meadows seem to encourage elk to stick around after they've eaten their fill. These small, scattered islands of prime feeding and resting ground are perfect places on which to focus your hunting attention when you're faced with a large expanse of forest.

Streamsides are obvious places in which to find wet meadows, but don't assume every stream will have a continuous meadow running along both banks. And because streams flow in canyon bottoms, elk may prefer to hang around moist sites higher up. Springs and seeps located along ridges and hillsides often produce small, wet meadows that get a lot of elk traffic. Also, look for swamps, ponds, and seasonal water holes that may be perched on high terraces.

The new 7.5-minute topographic maps are helpful in pinpointing the whereabouts of tributary streams, springs, and small forest openings that may be associated with meadows. Because these limited areas of superior elk habitat are usually scattered throughout the forest, a detailed map can also help you design a specific hunting route that links a number of wet meadows together.

One advantage to hunting these moist areas is that you can tell immediately from the presence or absence of tracks in the wet ground whether elk are using them or not. But where the surrounding forest is thick, you can almost bet that wet meadows will produce good elk hunting.

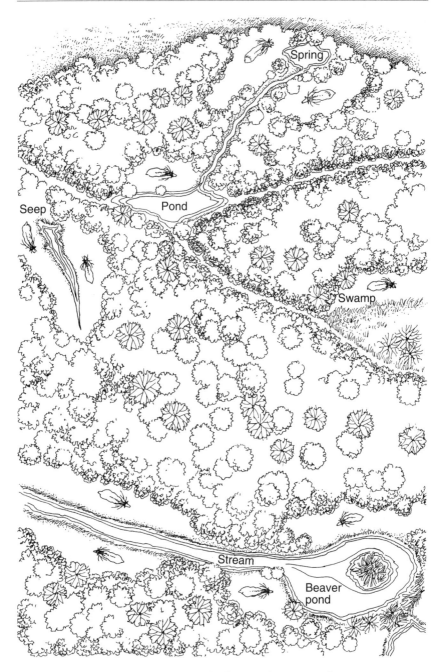

Use maps to locate moist features that attract elk.

Chapter 9

Up On Top

Whenever elk season opens I think back to an autumn back-packing trip I made with a friend about twenty years ago. We were hiking a divide trail that followed high ridges for fifty miles through Idaho's backcountry. Evenings, after we'd set up camp, we would sit and watch shadows lengthen across the drainage heads below us. And into those open bowls on either side of the divide elk would come by the dozens. It happened every evening and again in the morning in whatever drainage we happened to be camped above.

"What a place to hunt elk," we said to each other over and over again.

In the years since that time I've found that hunting up high certainly can be the place to find elk, especially bulls. But there are also a few drawbacks to this kind of hunt—not the least of which is getting up there and getting your elk out.

Terry Lonner, an elk researcher and friend, says anyone who hunts elk way up around timberline and above ought to take along a psychiatrist and a priest. But he also admits that big bulls will go to great heights to get away from hunting pressure. Last year another friend, hunting at 10,000 feet early in the season, came across a group of twelve elk; eight were legal bulls.

The presence of elk at higher elevations has a lot to do with the weather. On a typical opening day in the West, elk are widely dispersed from 5,500 to 10,000 feet provided early storms haven't driven them out of the high country. Once hunting season gets under full swing, though, the pressure from lower elevations pushes many elk up higher until weather forces them back down again.

So as long as the weather holds in the high country, some elk are going to stay up there. And those elk are likely to be bulls. According to Terry Lonner, "The bigger bulls will be working the more rugged terrain. These stag groups will commonly be found in more unfertile areas, and those, very often, are at high elevations. If you're looking for big bulls, that's a good place to go through at least mid-season, depending on the weather."

Ironically, the security of these high bowls and drainage heads doesn't come in the form of physical cover, since trees are sparse and stunted except on north slopes. And often elk remain well above timberline. Lonner notes, "It's the remoteness and the lack

Hunting the high country isn't easy, but sights like this are a real possibility.

of hunting pressure that provide the security. Let's face it, most hunters don't like to negotiate that miserable terrain up there."

But security isn't the only attraction that keeps bulls up high during the hunting season. In early fall, there is usually better forage production up high than down below. While the grasses and sedges at lower elevations are already dried out, growth in the high country is still going on because lingering snow cover has delayed its start in early summer.

"There's still good forage up there out in the open and in the timber as well because that timber on south slopes is sparse enough to allow sunlight to come through. So you have pretty good growing conditions," says Lonner.

While the quality of food in the high country is as good or better than at lower elevations, the quantity is not as great. Interspersed with rock outcroppings and talus slopes, forage is more scattered and patchy. To compensate for this, elk move around more in the course of a day. And most of that moving around is done in very sparse timber or in alpine bowls and meadows above timberline. Even when elk aren't feeding they can often be found bedded down out in the open well into the morning because they aren't used to being hunted at these elevations. This lack of wariness, combined with their increased mobility in a habitat that offers sparse cover, makes high-country elk more vulnerable to any hunter willing to make the effort to hunt them there.

If all this is sounding like the kind of elk hunting you should have gotten into years ago, remember the words of Terry Lonner: "The hardest part of hunting elk at high elevations is getting up there. You gotta have a lot of guts and be stupid."

While Terry might be prone to hyperbole, there are some definite reasons why most hunters don't hunt at timberline and above. Many feel that a hunt of this nature requires the use of a guide, and for anyone who isn't at ease in the backcountry, a

Barren, rocky ridgelines often make solitary bulls easy to spot.

guide is certainly in order. But do-it-yourself high-country elk hunts are possible if you're a competent camper and pathfinder.

Realistically, it may mean packing camping gear in for five or six miles and setting up a cold camp in areas where firewood is not easily found. It requires a definite investment of time and energy, if not money. And, of course, as in any elk hunt, there are no guarantees. Still, the bulls are up there.

One thing you have in your favor is the fact that you don't have to climb to the highest ridges to hunt these timberline elk. On that backpacking trip twenty years ago, I had a great view of all kinds of elk bedded and feeding in the bowls below me. But to actually hunt them from that high divide would have been difficult. In most cases, the elk were too far away to shoot, and to have worked down off the divide out in the open and over steep boulder fields would have undoubtedly alerted the animals to my presence.

"You're better off scoping from a lower point," Lonner says. "If you're up high looking down, very often the elk are too far away to shoot. But if you're glassing from an 8,000-foot bowl or from a subalpine valley and you see elk up above, very often there are elk in between those higher elk and where you are. And while you're going for the elk up above, you can run into the other elk. When you're up high, you're on top of the world, but then you've got to get down to the elk."

Terry's advice reminds me of the time I awoke at dawn in a camp my partner and I had made in a little swale at treeline in the northern Rockies. Above camp there was a hummock of glacial debris that made a perfect observation point to scope the spacious grassy bowl beyond. Before I'd even sipped from the cup of coffee I'd taken up there with me, I spotted elk high on the far flanks of the bowl. They appeared to be almost half a mile away, but I decided I could close most of that distance undetected by using the terrain as cover. Leaving my partner to keep an eye on the elk and give me hand signals if they started to move, I began my stalk.

I couldn't have gone more than a few hundred yards when I poked my head over a small rise and came eyeball to eyeball with five bulls. They'd been hidden from my view by a dip in the landscape. Had I taken the time to sip my first cup of coffee, they might have moved close enough for me to have shot one from my breakfast table.

Patience is definitely a virtue when you're hunting elk way up there. You'll want to spend most of your time sitting and scanning the surroundings with binoculars or a spotting scope. Because much of the terrain is open, movement—other than carefully stalking specific animals—may inadvertently spook any elk in the area. So when you make camp, do it with an eye for a nearby observation point: a knoll or ridge, even a big boulder that will give you a clear view of the high country elk are likely to use.

Once you've spotted elk, don't rush into action without considering your options. If you remain undetected, the elk aren't going to run off. In fact, chances are fifty-fifty they'll come closer. So check the lay of the land. Examine routes where the terrain will allow someone to move in on the game unseen. If you're hunting with partners, which you should have in rugged, remote country, have one person stay in place while the others attempt to approach the elk from different directions. Have your stationary man give hand signals—worked out ahead of time—that let you know where to move and what the elk are up to. By making a very slow and calculated approach you may well get a shot at an elk that is standing still or even lying down.

The main advantage to having several people in on the hunt, however, is that someone is still likely to get a shot if the elk spook. And that someone might just be the man left at the observation point.

When elk get nervous in the high country they head down. They may first move up and around, but they're eventually going to end up coming down into the protection of the trees. And if you're below them they may pass within range before they get into the trees. For this reason it's a good idea to identify the most obvious exit routes elk will take from open terrain into forested areas below. Whenever possible they'll take the path of least resistance.

The flight response of spooked elk can easily be a mile. And you can bet they aren't going to settle down until they've reached cover. So following elk in the high country once they've gone on the run is usually a futile undertaking. They'll head for the north slopes where trees are the densest and the downfalls are a jungle of pick-up sticks. Plan to hunt high-country elk out in the open.

Once you have an elk down, the hard part of the hunt will suddenly loom large. "You bone a mature bull out and you're looking at two hundred pounds of meat. And then you want to bring out the cape, the antlers . . ." Terry Lonner chuckles at this point. "I just don't hunt elk in the high country anymore."

All this weight can be packed out, of course, but it may take several trips for three men to get out one elk. The quarters can

Once you've located a bull in the open, take your time and consider all escape routes before choosing the best path to get into position for a shot.

even be dragged out with the hide left on if the terrain isn't too rocky. Or you may be able to make arrangements to have a packer haul your trophy out with a horse. Hunting high-country elk can get complicated at this point, there's no doubt. But if you haven't tried it, you ought to, at least once. Do it soon, though, as it's a sport for younger hunters.

A COW-ELK COALITION

Back in 1960 the Montana Department of Fish, Wildlife & Parks (MDFWP) purchased 7,067 acres of blue-bunch wheatgrass and Idaho fescue above the Madison River in southwest Montana. Called the Wall Creek Wildlife Management Area, the land was intended to provide winter range for elk, with no domestic cattle allowed. For over twenty years, however, elk left the management area in the spring to feed on greener grass that grew on adjacent private ranches. And come fall, cattle abandoned the national forest grazing allotments located above Wall Creek and muscled their way down through fences to eat grass intended for wintering elk.

Clearly, there was a problem.

The MDFWP, the U.S. Forest Service, and the Wall Creek Stock Association (a group of local ranchers) met in 1982 to work on a solution. They agreed to attempt a coordinated management plan that would reduce elk/cattle competition while improving forage conditions for all. After six years of experimentation, the result is a rest-rotation grazing system that crosses ownership boundaries and benefits approximately 1,200 elk, 700 domestic cows, and hunters and ranchers alike.

Under the system, ten pastures, separated by electric fences, are arranged in elevations ranging from 5,600 to 9,000 feet with three pastures at low elevations, three at mid elevations, and four at high elevations. Each year, according to a precise schedule, one set of three pastures is grazed by cows that move up in elevation during the growing season—before elk move onto their winter range. Each of the ten pastures

Continued on next page

gets two years of vegetative rest following one year of grazing.

Cows that graze in the spring at low elevations clean off dead plant litter that elk have found unpalatable in the past. And by the end of September—the time when cattle had been pushing at the management area's fences—all cows are back on private ranchland for the winter.

Managers, ranchers, and hunters have been pleased with the results. "We're no longer in an adversarial role with our ranching neighbors," says Kurt Alt, wildlife biologist with the MDFWP. "We're working with them and they're working with us. It's a win-win situation."

And it may very well be a win-win situation throughout the West. Four other states have already shown an interest in Wall Creek's cow-elk coalition. It may become a model worth imitating for those attempting to maintain elk herds while simultaneously keeping ranchers in business—and their lands free from subdivision sprawl.

Chapter 10

CLOSE TO HOME

When my friend George arrived on my doorstep to go elk hunting, he was prepared to head for the highest peaks in search of his game. He had flown over the mountains of Montana on his way in, and when he didn't see snow, he figured the elk would be at the highest elevations. George had climbed flights of stairs with bricks in a backpack to prepare for mountain climbing. He looked at me squinty-eyed when I told him we'd spend opening day at the top of a knoll three hundred feet above where we'd leave the Jeep.

At the beginning of hunting season, many elk are at low elevations. As hunting pressure builds, they climb only enough to escape the worst of the pressure. In the mild weather of early season, you'll find elk at 5,000 to 10,000 feet. They live at different elevations so as not to eat up their food supply. Even as hunting pressure pushes them higher, there are always some elk at lower elevations, and you may have to climb only a little bit farther than other hunters to find them. For example, seventy to eighty elk stayed at 5,500 to 6,000 feet for the entire first week of the season where I hunted last year. This was in spite of heavy hunting pressure and unusually warm weather.

Consider hunting low at the start of the season instead of the more popular season ending, when many hunters feel harsh weather will be in their favor. The beginning of the season gives you the advantage of surprise. You can scout and locate elk before they're disturbed and plan specific strategies for opening morning when elk will be confused and may just mill around instead of running off.

After the first days of hunting, though, the elk adjust. They change their routines and disappear from the most accessible areas. They use their home range differently, and although they avoid areas that lack security, they rarely abandon their home range altogether. In fact, the highest densities of elk during most of the hunting season where I hunt in Montana are between the mid elevations of 7,000 to 8,000 feet. It's a range that's passed up by a lot of hunters, especially in mild weather, because they figure that spooked elk are always going to use high elevation as security.

By the third day of our hunt the elk had moved higher. So when George missed a chance at a bull at 6,000 feet, he was ready to put his bricks-and-backpack training to good use. However, I saw no reason to get out the climbing ropes and the pitons just yet.

"Lots of hunters are going to be pushing around between 8,000 and 9,000 feet, especially with the lack of snow up there," I told my friend. "Even more hunters are going to hang low hoping to bag a straggler."

After the first week of the season, it's a good rule of thumb not to start seriously hunting elk until you're a half mile away from any road that's being used. Elk avoid roads that have even occasional traffic, and the sparser the cover near the road, the farther away they'll move.

You don't always have to head up high for bulls. With some scouting, you can often find them at much lower elevations.

Closed roads are another matter. On national forest lands, many logging roads are closed to motorized traffic after logging operations are completed. Any national forest headquarters or district ranger station can provide travel plan maps detailing road closures for their area. These maps will help you locate areas where it's possible to hike to good elk hunting by way of closed roads.

Some experienced hunters like to hunt an area where there have been a lot of rifle shots. Once elk have overcome their initial season-opening confusion, though, they'll quickly move a mile after hearing a nearby gunshot. I know an instance of a radio-monitored elk moving two miles in fifteen minutes after hearing a gunshot. That leaves a lot of hunters stomping around in the woods by themselves.

In mid elevations, elk often use steepness instead of remoteness for their security, and you can reach most parts of these areas

In areas with high pressure, it's sometimes possible to find elk that are on the move to escape other hunters. (USFWS)

in the Rockies via logging roads. Elk hide in small groups within easy reach on the abrupt east slope where steepness and heavy timber keep most hunters away. I suggested to George that we work the top halves of side ridges branching off the east slope. It was country I'd hunted before, and I knew elk took refuge there during hunting season. Besides, I'd just purchased a 7.5-minute topographical map on which one mile sprawled over a whole two and a half inches of detailed contour lines. These maps are available for most of the Rockies. The large detail gives you a perspective on the landscape that's impossible to gain in the field.

These maps also may reveal hidden areas where elk might feel secure, and show you how to get to them most easily. For example, by studying the map of the ridge I thought I knew so well, I discovered a draw I'd never known was there. I also found that a terrace I'd never hunted because of its apparently terrible access had an easy hidden passage that became clear on the map.

We tried the terrace and I laughed at how easily it could be reached once I knew how. Although fresh elk beds and droppings covered the area, we saw no elk, or hunters. I've since returned to the terrace and found elk but have yet to find hunters there, though it's a scant half mile from a paved road.

George's bricks-and-backpack training wasn't entirely wasted, though. The hidden east-slope draw I'd discovered on the map was very steep, and we approached it from the bottom where we could gain access on a little-used logging spur. An hour later, when we eased up on the six-pointer bedded by the roots of a toppled fir, George had become a believer in the benefits of hunting elk within reach. The pull-out was less than grueling, and given the pitch of the slope, even the lack of snow didn't call for heroic efforts.

Snow, of course, is a factor that can bring elk within reach. As temperatures drop and snow piles up at higher elevations, elk congregate at lower elevations. With deep snow above and

Snow eventually forces elk down from the high country, but hunting pressure from below can leave them hanging in a fairly narrow elevation band.

hunting pressure below, the elevation band in which elk seek security may become quite narrow.

Hunting this band effectively means working the steeper terrain and thicker timber often found on east and north slopes. These don't have to be remote spots. Use the 7.5-minute topos for a real eye-opener; they're useful even in terrain you think you know. And head for the inconspicuous gullies and terraces where elk are often bunched up within your reach but just off the edges of the heavy hunting pressure.

Order topographic maps via the Internet at http://store.usgs.gov or over the phone by calling the U.S. Geological Survey in Denver, Colorado, at 303-236-5900 and asking for an index of topographic maps for the state of your choice. Sporting goods and general outdoor stores usually carry these maps for their surrounding areas as well.

Chapter 11

FORECASTING ELK
WHEREABOUTS

Terry and I were talking over coffee and pie on July 1 when he told me where I'd find elk come fall hunting season.

"They're going to be spread out from up in the goat rocks all the way down to winter range. They'll have a real wide distribution, and the likelihood of bumping into an elk will be better than most years."

Someone eavesdropping on Terry's prediction might have figured he was a clairvoyant or a shaman or merely a nut. But as I mentioned in an earlier chapter, Terry is a wildlife biologist whose specialty is elk.

"The weather we've had this winter and spring is really going to influence the distribution of elk through the summer and into the fall. We had a lot of snowpack going into spring, and then we got all that cold that delayed the snowmelt. So the ground's still pretty moist. The vegetation's in good shape all over the elk range."

The weather conditions that occur months before elk season opens have a great deal to do with where elk are likely to be found in the fall. A careful look at precipitation and temperatures from winter through summer and even into fall can tell you about the state of elk forage and, therefore, about elk whereabouts during hunting season.

A snowy winter combined with a cold spring, for example, can delay plant and shrub development in the spring, which means that vegetation is still succulent and nutritious in open areas come fall. Consequently, elk may spend much more time

Weather conditions throughout the spring and summer influence available forage come hunting season. Take this into account when planning your next outing.

than usual grazing in meadows and on open hillsides during hunting season, giving you a definite place to look for them.

While a harsh winter and spring keeps elk widely distributed and feeding out in the open during the fall, a mild, dry winter and spring has the opposite effect. In studies of Rocky Mountain elk in northeastern Oregon, a spring with below normal snowfall caused plant growth to start two to three weeks earlier than normal. As a result, the elks' peak use of grasses and forbs on open grassland came a month earlier than the previous year, and the elk also shifted their feeding activities from grassland to forest habitats a month earlier.

"In droughty years," Terry told me, "elk are more concentrated in moist sites at drainage heads and along creeks and streams. And if you know where elk are going to congregate because of what weather has done to their forage, you can really hit the mother lode."

"The fall of 1988 is a good example. We'd had a terrible drought for almost three years, and we wound up with the fires in Yellowstone Park. That year's was the highest elk kill ever in Montana. A tough snowy fall in the high country combined with the poor forage over most of their range brought all the elk down along the river drainages looking for something green to eat."

But dry summers don't always bring elk down low. If the high county remains snow free, elk typically find forage desiccated in alpine meadows and bowls, but they may still have good pickings on forested north slopes. Here, both the aspect and the tree cover help delay plant phenology until later in the season. In addition, these slopes hold moisture longer and nurture late-season growth. Elk gather on these high-country sites until forage gives out or snow and cold drive them to milder conditions at lower elevations.

On a midsummer hiking trip along an alpine divide, I can remember looking down into drainage heads and seeing elk feeding in the high meadows. I was sure I'd found an elk hunter's heaven. And I knew if I could be back up on that divide on opening day I'd have no trouble getting one of the big bulls I'd seen.

I was wrong.

I did arrange to be back on that divide for the first day of elk hunting. But I didn't get a bull. I didn't even see an elk until I bumbled into a mess of them munching grass in the timber on a north slope I'd used to get back to my truck. If I'd known that the hot summer weather was going to move the elk to those protected slopes I might have gotten a bull after all. As it was, I just waded into the herd like a sow at a church social.

Under ideal conditions, elk may hold up in the high country feeding out in the open through the entire hunting season. "I don't know if you remember '75 and '76," Terry said over an empty coffee cup. "Seventy-five was a very delayed winter, a long winter. I mean it lasted until May. And I remember over in the Big Hole walking on snowdrifts at 8,000 feet in early July. The drifts were fifteen feet high. Normally, they're totally gone by then. Well, the elk really didn't get into the high country until mid-July, and the plant growth was just getting underway. Then we had a very mild fall. Well, we were finding radio-collared elk on summer range at 9,000 feet in the middle of January!"

Perhaps the longest-lasting weather phenomenon to influence elk whereabouts is the thunderstorm. Electrical storms set forest fires every summer in the West. In a year of normal moisture, the size of those burns may be only a few acres. But when the weather has been really dry, hundreds or thousands of acres may burn. The typical effect of those burns is to provide nutrients to the soil which prompt renewed and vigorous growth of ground cover for one to three years afterward. The new growth of both grasses and browse is highly digestable and nutritious for elk—up to 50 percent more nutritious than before the fire.

In areas where thick forest prevents good understory growth, fires can open up the tree canopy and spur on the growth of grasses, forbs, and shrubs. So an area of a few acres or hundreds of acres that was once uninhabited by elk can be turned into a favorite elk hangout by the effects of one thunderstorm.

By making note of recent burn locations in your area, you can locate elk-hunting hotspots with a great deal of accuracy. And don't ignore little one- and two-acre burns. They can draw elk as easily as the big ones. (See chapter 24 for more information on the effect fire has on how elk use their home range.)

While looking at the weather that occurs months or even years before hunting season arrives definitely allows you to forecast elk whereabouts during the season, conditions within weeks of the hunting season deserve close consideration too. The early fall storms typical of September and October in the West's high country are usually greeted by elk hunters with much ballyhoo because it's thought the snow will drive the elk down to lower elevations. And the elk often do respond temporarily to early snows by moving somewhat lower, but Indian summer can move in for weeks at a time after these storms.

The resulting high-country moisture, coming after dry summer months and followed by the return of warm weather, often produces fall regrowth of grasses at high elevations. But little or no regrowth may occur at lower elevations because they often don't get much moisture from these storms. Still, hunters often stay down low looking for elk that have moved lower for a few days only to return to the high country for the best forage around.

Many years ago, frustrated with the absence of elk where I thought they should have been pushed by early snows, I followed a ridgeline for miles back into the mountains. I'd gained almost 2,000 feet in elevation according to my topo map, and I was just about to head back down when I caught sight of a rump patch

Early mountain storms followed by warm weather can restart grass growth, allowing elk to stay up high longer into the hunting season.

through a screen of branches. A small meadow spread out below me on a side-ridge terrace, and eleven elk grazed there on what appeared to be badly desiccated grass.

After I'd downed one of the elk, I was able to take a close look at what they'd been eating. Through the crisp, brown weave of dried grasses, tender green shoots poked out. What appeared from a distance to be meager pickings was, in fact, an ideal meal. And it was that high-altitude fall regrowth that was keeping elk from where I thought they should be.

While fall regrowth can keep elk up high, heavy frosts can push them down into the timber even in the absence of much snow. Repeated frosts in alpine bowls and meadows makes grass and forbs limp, and they tend to mat close to the ground, making grazing difficult. When frosts are combined with some snowfall the effect on the vegetation can be much like trampling.

Looking at the high country from down in the foothills, you may assume that forage is still fine for elk feeding up above. Yet they may very well have moved into the cover of mid-elevation forests where the effects of frost are moderated by the tree canopy.

What becomes clear after you've observed the effects of weather conditions on elk whereabouts over a number of years is that certain conditions tend to concentrate elk in certain locations. Where they congregate will depend on where they can find the topography, the elevation, the aspect, and the vegetation that will best moderate the weather's negative influence on their forage.

As a forecaster of elk whereabouts you must always be asking yourself: How are this year's weather patterns going to influence the availability of fall elk forage and where is the best forage likely to be given those weather patterns?

To put an elk like this in your scope, it helps to know what conditions will be like in a variety of cover types at any given time. (USFWS)

If it has been an early and dry summer, for example, most plants on open slopes will be desiccated by late summer, and elk may be congregated to feed in high, moist sites where snowbanks are still melting or where alpine streams and lakes still support green vegetation. More likely, though, they'll be on high north or east slopes where the forest canopy still keeps understory vegetation palatable.

Once you've determined the best places to find suitable forage, check these sites at dawn and dusk when elk are most likely to be feeding. But don't be discouraged if you don't find elk there immediately.

Elk specialist Terry Lonner notes, "Elk are high frequency, low intensity grazers. They just don't stand in one spot and mow the grass like cattle. They're very selective. In one feeding period of two hours they might walk a mile."

So if you've found signs of recent feeding in an area, you'll do well to stake it out for a day or two. The harder the weather conditions have been on overall forage availability, the more precious those niches of suitable forage will be and the more frequently elk will use them. Don't blow your chances of getting into a mother lode of elk by impatiently cruising through those areas.

This is a time when taking a stand for elk can be productive. They'll be on the move, and if there are limited areas of good forage, they'll be passing near where you wait sooner or later.

A final pointer from Lonner: "You will probably see the most dramatic effect of weather on elk distribution during a normal year. By early August vegetation at 7,000 feet and less is very dried out. And then you go up to 9,000 feet and it's succulent as all get out. That's when you're going to see the most dramatic differences in the development of vegetation at any given point in time." And that's when you're going to find elk in the high country at the beginning of hunting season.

But also remember that extreme cold and heavy snow in the high country during the hunting season is going to move most elk out of there no matter how green the grass may be. That is always the ultimate "now factor" in the long-range forecasting of elk whereabouts.

ELK FORECASTER

Seasonal Weather Conditions	Effects on Forage	Forecast for Elk Whereabouts
Snowy winter and cold spring	Delayed plant/shrub development = succulent forage in open areas into fall	Open meadows and hillsides
Mild, dry winter and spring	Early plant/shrub development = dry forage in most areas by late summer	Under forest cover, especially north and east slopes
Drought	Widespread desiccation of vegetation	Moist sites in drainage heads and along streams
Early, wet fall followed by Indian summer	Fall grass regrowth	Higher elevations
Early, heavy frosts at higher elevations	Dried and matted grass and broadleaf plants	Mid-elevation forests
Electrical storms	Local forest fires	Freshly burned areas, especially 1 to 3 years after fire
Average year	Low- to mid-elevation brown-out by August, but high elevations remain green	Hunt high

Chapter 12

BREAKING WITH TRADITION

Many of our hunting strategies are based on an elk herd's traditional use of the land. Elk have well-established summer and winter ranges, and they use the same travel lanes each season to move between these traditional ranges, but as elk populations have increased, some elk have started breaking with tradition, moving away from established ranges to colonize new terrain.

With the help of enlightened management practices, most established elk herds have increased in population, some by well over 100 percent in the last fifteen years. With these increases comes more competition within a herd for food and cover, and eventually some elk begin looking for greener pastures. Their departures from areas of traditional use invariably come in the spring and summer when the social stability of a herd seems to be at its weakest. At this time, as many as twenty-five to thirty elk split from the main herd and start using areas that have not been elk haunts in the recent past.

Typically, these newly colonized areas are adjacent to forested terrain that has been used by elk within the past century. These

When an elk herd reaches capacity on a given range, which is now happening in many areas of the West, some members of the group may move into new areas. (USFWS)

areas are most often at lower elevations in open treeless country covered with sagebrush. Recent instances of lowland colonization have occurred in Washington, Idaho, and Montana. Ironically, elk appear to be moving back to habitats they were forced to leave by nineteenth-century settlement of the West.

This treeless grassland is well-suited for elk. Their social behavior can accommodate the use of new and different terrain by some members of the herd as the need arises. In addition, their physiological makeup also enables them to use a greater variety of habitats than we have come to expect. And colonist elk show as much fidelity to their newly colonized areas as the main herd does to its traditional habitat.

Despite their adaptive capabilities, however, most colonist elk return to their main herd's traditional habitat when faced with weather extremes. For example, although small groups of elk in Montana split from the main herd to spend summer and fall in lowland sagebrush, they always rejoin the herd on its traditional range during harsh winters. Similarly, during the 1988 Montana drought, a group of elk that had established its own summer range rejoined the main herd in its traditional summer range in wetter drainage heads.

The recent growth in elk populations and the resulting colonization have several implications for elk hunters. First, while most hunters are heading for the forested higher elevations, it may be possible to find small groups of elk hunkered down on lower borders where grassland and timberland meet, in areas that are generally ignored by most hunters. Second, the tendency of elk to bail out of newly colonized ranges when the weather gets nasty suggests that traditional areas—such as winter range—provide optimum satisfaction to elk during harsh times. And that's where the highest concentrations of elk will be.

THE SINGLE-FILE SPREAD

Hunters often moan about how elk move so fast and so far. What a lot of hunters don't realize is that elk often move around them in circles or parallel to the path they have just taken. The elk you spook now may well appear to head away from you, only to swing around and cross the spot where you were standing ten minutes ago. In addition, elk don't always head uphill when spooked; they frequently move downhill, building up speed before cutting off in a different direction.

The hunting tactic that takes advantage of this elk behavior is something I call the "single-file spread." It can be done with two or more hunters walking single file over the same route spread about three hundred yards apart. The tactic can involve continuous walking or a combination of stopping and walking. The five specific scenarios of hunter and elk movement described here have happened to me numerous times. Unfortunately, I wasn't always prepared for them.

Two of these situations may occur in the morning, when elk are feeding in open, grassy areas. First, as elk move up from feeding on open foothills to reach the cover of timber, a lone hunter may intercept this movement only to have the elk veer away and enter the timber behind or ahead of him. The singe-file spread, set up perpendicular to expected elk movement into timber, can pay off here.

In the second scenario, elk caught feeding on an open hillside often circle around behind the hill to make their es-

Continued on next page

cape down the opposite side. Three or four hunters spread out to partially encircle a hill that is a likely morning feeding ground can take advantage of this elk escape tactic.

The other three common elk escape ploys occur later in the day after elk have already taken to the timber for security. Elk may attempt to keep sidehill timber or timbered ridges between you and them, circling around behind timber as you move up from the other side. A hunter following the same route some distance behind you may connect with the elk as they loop back around the timber.

Elk also like to move downhill parallel to you on one side of timber while you're moving uphill on the other side. These elk/hunter movements can also be reversed. In either case, the single-file spread gives the hunters behind the lead hunter a chance at a shot through sparse timber or intervening openings. The same is true when you move up a side ridge and elk escape by moving downhill in the draw parallel to you.

In all of these situations, spacing between hunters should be determined by the relative size of the landforms and the timber stands near your hunting site.

Understanding Behavior

Chapter 13

SCOUTING

The heavy snows had yet to descend on the high country, and my usual hunting companions had declined my invitation to an early season elk hunt. There wouldn't be any elk in the area I'd suggested, they said, despite my assurances to the contrary. And the fact that I hadn't actually *seen* elk during my preseason scouting trips was the clincher that found them at home and me hunting alone on opening day.

What I had seen during my scouting trips were the telltale signs of elk. The shredded bark on several saplings and the trampled mud of a fresh wallow indicated that there was a bull elk in the area that was getting ready for rut. So there I sat in heavy brush at the edge of the clearing where I'd found the wallow. The battered saplings were within sight at the far side of the meadow. After two hours of waiting I was beginning to wonder if my hunch was right. But five minutes later, when a five-point bull trotted into the clearing, I had become a believer in signs—elk signs.

Many hunters consider elk to be North America's most coveted game animal, yet many of those same hunters spend days and sometimes weeks in the field without seeing elk. The reason for this may be that they neglect to look and listen for the telltale signs that elk leave.

Elk tracks, scat, chews, beds, antlers, rubs, wallows, and sounds are all indicators that let you know where the elk are and what they're doing. By finding and interpreting these signs you greatly increase your chances of getting an elk, particularly when you're hunting without the aid of a professional guide.

SCAT

When snow is absent and the ground is such that it doesn't easily hold a track, elk droppings are a better indication of the animal's presence in the area. In the fall months when the elk's diet consists of dried vegetation, its droppings are acorn-shaped pellets about three-quarters of an inch long, and they look as if they're composed of pressed sawdust. They can be distinguished from moose scat, at this time of year, because they're not as smooth or rounded. Fresh droppings appear moist and shiny while old ones look dry and dull, although environmental conditions also play a role in judging age.

Droppings will often be found where elk have been feeding and where they've bedded down. So it's wise to remain in an area where fresh scat occurs. During mornings and late afternoons post yourself just below a high point overlooking the surrounding terrain. During the day, cover the area very slowly on foot, paying particular attention to heavy timber where elk may be bedded down.

CHEWS

Elk are primarily grazers, but when early snows cover the ground they are sometimes forced to browse on available trees. Aspen bark is preferred, and where chew marks appear in moist bark that still shows green around the edges, elk have been feeding there recently. Tracks in the snow combined with the chew marks will help you determine more accurately when the elk have been there. Fresh signs would suggest that it's wise to keep an eye on these feeding grounds in the morning and afternoon but to follow the tracks during the middle of the day.

BEDS

Depressions appearing in grass or snow often indicate that elk have bedded down there. The only way to verify this is by the presence of elk tracks or droppings nearby. When these signs are fresh the chances are good that elk may be staying in the vicinity for a time. They may return to these bedding grounds during the middle of the day, making them good areas to still-hunt during that time.

ANTLERS

Bulls drop their antlers in the spring. So if you begin to discover shed elk horns in a particular area, you can be sure that you've come upon an elk wintering ground. These telltale signs are especially helpful for late season hunting. At that time snow in the high country may be getting deep, forcing elk to move down to inhabit wintering areas. Since elk most often move as a herd to such places, your chances of seeing a lot of elk are very good. On several occasions I've come upon elk migrating to wintering grounds. It's a sight to behold. During this kind of mass movement the cows and yearlings come down first, with the old bulls taking up the rear. Waiting for those bulls is an exciting proposition, you can be sure.

RUBS

As bull elk start to prepare for the rutting season they scrape the velvet from their horns by rubbing them against saplings. Young spruce and pine that average about three inches in diameter are

Scouting for clues about how and when elk use cover will help you come home with a trophy like this one. (Jay Cassell)

their favorite rubbing trees. And when used for this purpose, the tree will have broken branches and bark shredded from its trunk to a height of five or six feet. When the bark is still moist and pliable you know the bull has been there recently.

My opening-day five-point bull left just such a tree as one of his calling cards, and other elk have done the same over the years. The bonus value of this particular sign is that it indicates more than just elk; it indicates bull elk. And where several of these battered trees exist fairly close to one another the chances are good that a single bull has adopted the area as his rutting territory. That means you should adopt the same area as your prime hunting territory.

WALLOWS

As rutting season progresses, bulls will find a soft, damp place in the earth where they stomp, roll, and urinate in a kind of mating ritual. These wallows appear as muddy, churned-up depressions surrounded by elk tracks. They're an important find for the elk hunter because a bull usually returns to a wallow once it's established. This kind of hunting is for the patient at heart because it means sitting and waiting, sometimes for days, for the bull to return to take another mud bath. If you don't have that kind of patience, the presence of a fresh wallow will at least indicate a good area to hunt on foot.

SOUNDS

Grunts and snorts are emitted by male and female elk when they're alarmed or surprised. Several years ago while hunting thick timber, I was startled by the loud snort of a cow elk that arose from her bed twenty yards from where I was walking. Had she not snorted, I probably wouldn't have seen her. Had she been a bull, the hunt would have been over.

Bugling is the most exciting telltale sign of all because it says a bull elk is present *right now.* This is the time you might want to use your own elk call to imitate the bugle of a young bull. When done successfully your call will bring in an old bull looking for the challenger to his territory. He may come trotting through the trees with his head held high or he might ghost slowly through the brush. Either way, it's an adrenaline-pumping experience. (See chapter 19 for more information on bugling and the rut.)

Actually seeing elk is only part of any elk hunt, and it's usually the briefest part. The majority of most hunts is spent out of sight of elk. That is why it's so important to keep an eye out for their signs. By knowing what to look for and where to look for it, and by knowing how to interpret what you find, you'll know where to find those elk. Obviously, one of the best signs you can find is tracks, and we'll deal with those in the next chapter.

Chapter 14

ALL ABOUT TRACKING

Elk easily travel a mile or two to keep out of trouble, and they'll keep on the move even when seriously wounded. So if you want to be a good elk hunter, you ought to be a good elk tracker. Becoming a good elk tracker is more than identifying elk tracks and following them. It's being able to identify and follow the clues given by antler tracks, beds, urine and scat, hair and blood, gait and course. It's a matter of knowing the significance of the number and size of tracks you find together. And it's learning the trick of aging tracks by more than a rough guess.

INDIVIDUAL TRACKS

Individual elk tracks are your starting point. Elk have quite blocky two-part hooves, averaging 4 to 4½ inches long by 3 to 3½ inches wide with rounded tips, in contrast to the pointed tips of most deer tracks.

Behind the broad imprint of an elk's cloven hoof you will sometimes see the smaller imprint of the two dewclaws, especially if the elk is running or if it's walking in sand, mud, or snow.

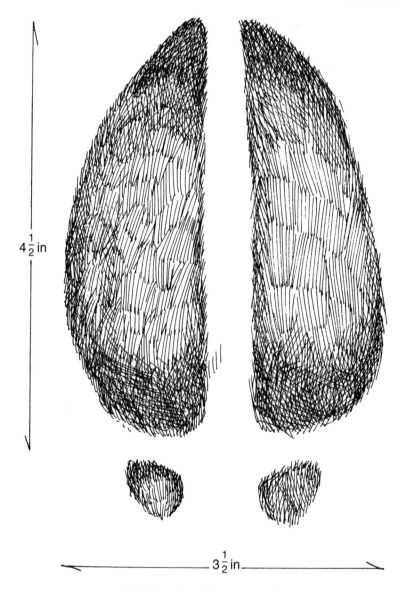

$4\frac{1}{2}$ in

$3\frac{1}{2}$ in

Bull elk track with dewclaw visible.

Primitive mammals had five clawed toes that, through time, have been reduced in number, size, and shape. The elk's dewclaws are remnants of two of these clawed toes, which give rise to the name.

The ability to distinguish front hooves from rear hooves can be important when tracking. The dewclaws of an elk's front feet are closer to the hooves than those of the rear feet. Also, the front hooves are somewhat larger than the rear hooves because of the additional neck and head weight they must carry. And these front hooves splay more when an elk is running or going downhill.

SIMILAR TRACKS

While confusion between deer and elk tracks is unlikely because of the deer's considerably smaller size, it is possible to confuse elk tracks with those of moose or even domestic cattle where grazing and elk habitat overlap. A moose track is larger, narrower, and more pointed than an elk track. While big—averaging five to six inches long and four to five inches wide—it appears more delicate, less blocky than an elk print. Where confusion over the owner of a track persists, check for pellet droppings to help in identification.

After elk have been eating the drier forage typically available during hunting season, their pellets tend to be concave on one end and slightly pointed at the other. They measure ½ to ¾ inch and are dark brown to black in color. Fall moose pellets, on the other hand, are rounded at both ends, and their texture more closely resembles compacted sawdust because of their woody browse diet. They measure between ¾ and one inch and are a lighter brown than elk pellets.

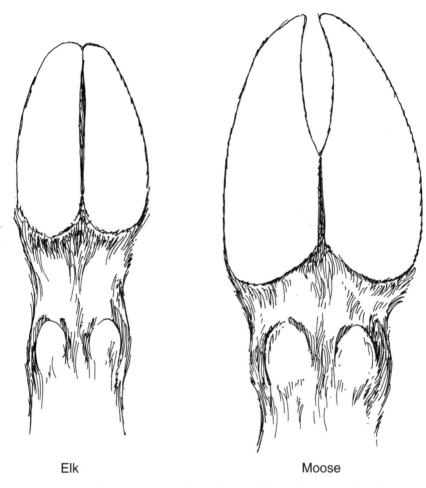

Elk   Moose

A moose hoof is larger and more pointed than an elk hoof (both shown from below).

When it comes to distinguishing an elk from a cow track, you'll notice that adult cattle tracks are big and square and quite distinctive. But a domestic calf may leave a print very similar to that of an adult elk, although somewhat smaller. When unsure, look for cow pies on the ground, a dead giveaway.

Elk Pellets

Moose Pellets

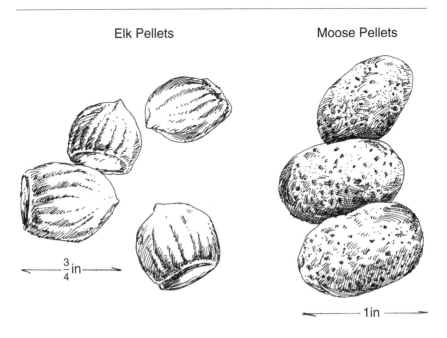

$\frac{3}{4}$in

1in

Domestic Calf

Adult Elk

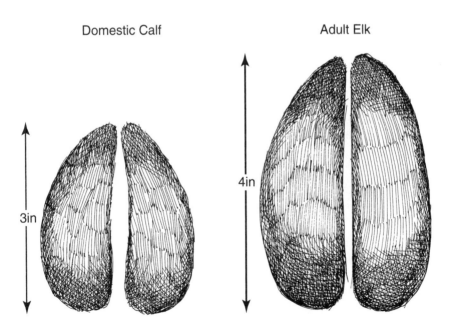

3in

4in

DETERMINING DIRECTION

Individual elk tracks can also tell you the direction the animal was headed. The pointiest ends of the individual hoof halves point in the direction of travel, as do the widest ends of the inside splay of the hoof halves. Finding the imprint of the dewclaws will also confirm the rear of the track and therefore the direction of travel.

When an elk travels in deep or powdery snow, these finer distinguishing features of a print may be obliterated. Then you'll have to depend on the track trough to tell the story of where the elk is going. Elk drag their hooves through the snow before actually putting them down on the ground and making a hoof print. The trough made by this dragging action as the hoof is coming down is longer and at a

Widest inside splay at front

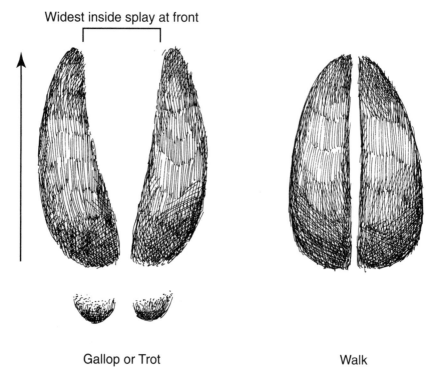

Gallop or Trot   Walk

Using a track to determine direction and gait.

Side view of track trough

Top view of track trough

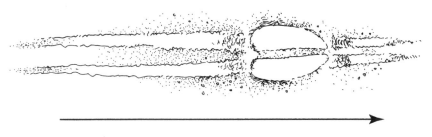

Determining direction in deep snow on flat ground.

shallower angle than the trough made as the hoof is being picked up. So the direction of travel will be toward the shorter, more angled trough when it appears on the flat or when going downhill.

Going uphill, an elk typically steps high and then drags its hoof forward. In this case, the longer, shallower trough will point in the direction of travel. Because of the possible confusion when trying to interpret hoof troughs on hillsides, use troughs as directional indicators only when you find them on flat ground.

AGING

After you've definitely identified an elk track, and in so doing also determined the animal's direction of travel, the next step is aging the track. If it was made several days earlier, the elk may very well be miles away. But a track made within a few hours of when you find it, or a track made in the evening and found the next morning, becomes part of a trail that is well worth following.

So many factors, over time, can influence the size, shape, texture, and appearance of tracks that it's impossible to discuss the effects of them all. Rain, snow, wind, frost, heat, and bitter cold transform tracks. Even gravity pulls at the edges of tracks, making them less crisp and distinctive as time goes by.

To learn the effects of all these factors on tracks made in different kinds of ground cover, the best teaching aid is an aging plot. It can be a patch of ground outside the tent of your elk camp, outside your motel room, or outside you own back door. In a spot that won't be disturbed but will be exposed to the effects of weather, make a print in sand, mud, dry dirt, or snow depending on what type of ground you expect to find where you hunt. You may want to try them all over a period of weeks.

You can make a print with your own foot, but I've found it more instructive to use an elk hoof where possible. One hour after making the first print, make another one nearby. And then make additional prints at 3, 6, 12, and 24 hours, or in some similar progression. Each time you make a new print notice the changes in the prints you've already made. Remember the weather changes that have occurred since the prints were made and observe the influences they've had on the tracks.

Maybe the wind that came up last night but was gone this morning blew sand in last night's track. Or perhaps yesterday's tracks are now filled with big, flaky frost made by this morning's dropping temperature.

By making an aging plot on a regular basis throughout the hunting season, your ability to age tracks accurately in the field will be greatly improved.

WHAT ELSE TRACKS REVEAL

A few individual tracks will tell you that an elk has been in the area and moving in a certain direction a given number of hours

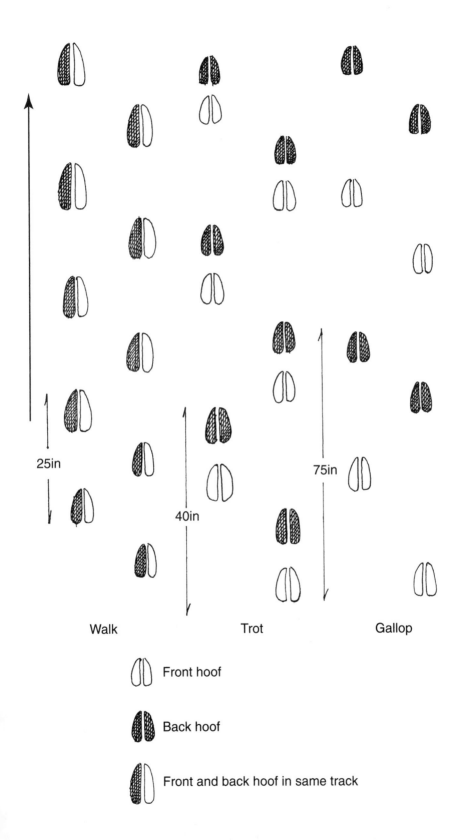

25in

40in

75in

Walk　　　　　Trot　　　　　Gallop

Front hoof

Back hoof

Front and back hoof in same track

ago. But you'll need to look at a trail of tracks to discover how fast the elk was moving and its general frame of mind.

The three gaits used most often by an elk are the walk, the trot, and the gallop. The walk suggests that an elk is in no hurry to get away from an area. The trot indicates a desire to get out of an area but without real panic. (Unfortunately for hunters, an elk can maintain a trot for miles without tiring.) The gallop is a definite sign of wanting to leave in a hurry, but it is rarely sustained by an elk over long distances.

In both the walk and the trot the individual tracks are roughly the same distance apart, and the pattern they make is identical on both the left and the right side of the track. While walking, an elk often places its rear hooves in the same place or slightly off-set from where its front hooves have been. A trot is indicated by the rear hooves landing in front of the front hooves and by a greater spacing between tracks.

The gallop is not symmetrical like the walk and trot. The distance between individual tracks is uneven, and the pattern they make is not the same on the left and right side of the trail.

With all gaits, the greater the distance between tracks, the faster the movement.

TRAILING

The decision to follow a trail has to be based on many factors, including the track's age, the number of daylight hours remaining, and the sex of the animal, which is particularly important if you have a bull-only permit.

Determining sex from hoof tracks is not a sure thing, but other indicators may help. Generally, a mature bull's track is larger than a mature cow's track, but it's a fine and relative distinction. The number of trails in an area is a better guide. The

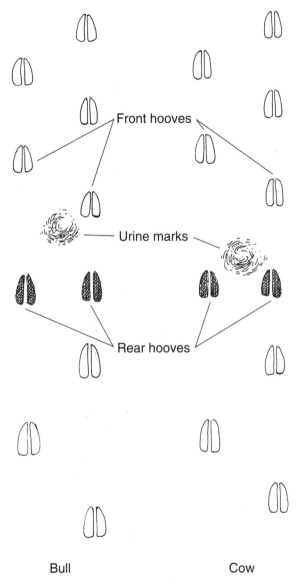

Front hooves

Urine marks

Rear hooves

Bull   Cow

Urine marks in relation to tracks are good indications of gender.

more trails you find together and the more variety they show in size, the greater the likelihood you've come across the tracks of a group of cows with their calves. A single trail, or even a double trail with large tracks, is a good indication of a solitary bull or a pair of bulls.

You may have to follow a trail for awhile before you find other signs to back up your initial speculations. Urine marks in relation to tracks and beds are good indications of sex. The urine mark of a bull appears well ahead of the rear hoof tracks and often just behind the rearmost front hoof track. A cow's urine mark, on the other hand, falls just in front of the rear hooves.

When you find a bed—an oval depression in snow, grass, or dirt—with a urine mark in the middle, you can be fairly sure it was made by a bull. A cow's bed will show the urine mark at one end. If there is no urine mark in the bed, but no other beds are present, it probably belongs to a bull. Numerous beds in the same area are usually made by cows.

By looking very closely at the immediate area—within two or three feet—surrounding a bed made in snow you may be able to find antler tracks made by a bedded bull as he stretched or scratched. These tracks appear as a thin groove or parallel grooves cut by antler points.

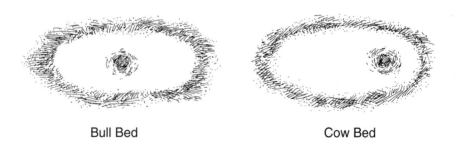

Bull Bed   Cow Bed

Antler tracks

Antler tracks

A bull makes antler tracks when stretching or scratching while in his bed.

HUNTING WHILE TRAILING

It should be clear that the actual process of following a trail comes only after you've made many educated guesses concerning the identity of the animal, its direction of travel, its frame of mind, and its sex. But, of course, following the trail is when you actually get down to hunting. And there are a number of hunting tactics that are dictated by the nature of the tracks and their trail.

When walking tracks that you know were made very recently, take a close look around without moving much more than your eyeballs. The elk may still be within sight of your position. If it isn't, you should follow the tracks very slowly.

Fresh trot tracks, or gallop tracks that turn into trot tracks, suggest that you may have spooked the elk yourself. In this case, it's better to hold tight for twenty or thirty minutes before setting off on the trail. This gives the elk time to realize it's not being chased, and it will typically to go back to feeding or bedding.

When you follow any trail, keep looking ahead as far as possible to see where the trail leads and where it may make any sudden change in course. Only look at the tracks at your feet when you want to check for a change in gait or when the distant course of the trail is unclear. When you keep your line of sight as far up the trail as you can, you're likely to see the elk as soon as it has a chance of seeing you.

A gallop or a trot trail can be followed quickly, but as soon as the trail indicates a walk, you should gear down to slow hunting. Keep an eye on the course of travel, too. As long as the trail appears in a fairly straight line it usually means the elk is not about to stop. When it begins to meander, the elk has probably started

If you came across the tracks of these bulls would you be able to discern when they passed through, their direction of travel, and how fast they were moving? (USFWS)

to feed or to look for a place to bed. It may be very close. This is the heart-pounding part of elk tracking, the actual sighting of an animal whose trail you may have been following for hours.

FINAL THOUGHTS

You may find yourself in the unenviable position of having to track a wounded elk. A blood trail can help determine the relative position of the wound. Check to see where the blood falls in relation to the front and rear hoof prints, and watch for drag marks that may indicate injury to or near a particular leg. If you find only a wad of hair with no blood, you may have just grazed the animal. But you should follow the trail for up to half a mile to see if blood does appear. Once you find a blood trail, keep on it until you find the elk or until it becomes clear that the animal wasn't seriously injured.

For the absolute best book on tracking—a book I have shamelessly borrowed from—get *A Field Guide to Mammal Tracking in North America*, by James Halfpenny, who authored a pocket guide to tracking as well, *Scats and Tracks of the Rocky Mountains*. I also recommend *A Field Guide to Tracking Animals in Snow*, by Louise R. Forrest, and that old standard, *A Field Guide to Animal Tracks*, by Olaus Murie.

Chapter 15

THOSE MADDENING, MEANDERING ELK

On a lucky day in winter, I might look through my living-room window and see four or five elk grazing on the south-western hillside. Walking and chomping, walking and chomping, they move through the sparse forest followed by more elk that materialize from the draw to the north. Soon, the entire hill is covered with thirty or forty slow-moving elk.

But before long the entire herd will have drifted across the landscape like smoke and, like smoke, will vanish without a trace. Elk may not appear on that hillside again for weeks, and if I don't happen to look out the window at just the right time, I will miss them. The whole process only takes about fifteen minutes—no rush, no panic, just sure and steady elk movement.

Ask an elk hunter what maddens him most about the game he pursues and he'll probably point to just that—movement. Since elk are always on the move, catching up with them has al-ways been a problem. But tracking studies are giving us a clearer picture of their daily movements, helping us understand why and how they move. And whether the animals are on their summer range, winter range, or in between, it's the idiosyncrasies of their meanderings that dictate hunting strategies and success.

First and foremost, elk move in order to fulfill their needs. Put another way, they move to stay comfortable, just as we do. An elk's first concern is food. This animal consumes ten to fifteen pounds of forage daily. Imagine tearing that much grass from the ground with just your teeth, and you'll get an idea of the time required for the process.

But first elk have to get to their feeding grounds. Because they prefer grass, their dining room is often out in the open, sometimes way out in the open. In fact, elk will readily move two to four miles from their daytime bedding areas in order to reach good patches of grass. Granted, this move—usually the major move of the day—often takes place under the cover of darkness

The availability of forage is typically the biggest factor in elk movement.

or dusk, but it's possible to intercept elk moving between feeding and bedding grounds, especially in the morning, which is the most active time of their day.

As was discussed in the last section, tracking studies show that elk move the most between 4 AM and 8 AM, and the least between 8 AM and 4 PM. So it's definitely to your advantage to be out there hunting by first light in the areas you know lie between elk feeding and bedding spots. The best tactic at this time of day is to stand hunt; leave the moving to the elk.

This first-light hunting can be as frustrating as it is rewarding. On numerous occasions, I've stood early-morning vigil waiting for a chance at elk moving off their feeding grounds. Sometimes, the elk you hear move by in the darkness are close enough to touch. At other times, their dim forms tease you as they pass by before legal shooting light. But by persistently waiting in the right spots, you will eventually catch a few stragglers or a whole herd that has stayed a little longer in the open to feed.

Don't rule out hunting elk in the middle of the day, however. Because of their relatively small rumens, elk need to eat frequently, taking lots of breaks in between meals to digest what they have consumed. So although they seek cover during the day, elk don't stay bedded down. In fact, they move an average of half a mile every couple of hours during the middle of the day, bedding for half an hour or so, then getting up to eat on the move again.

This frequent feeding routine is accompanied by a regular need for drinking water, especially in dry years and during the fall, when the moisture content of forage is reduced. At this time, major elk movement may be within half a mile of open water. So stake out those secluded seeps, springs, and sink holes.

While elk on the move are going to be more visible to you, they also may be more elusive, rarely in the same place today that they were yesterday. But they probably won't be far from where you saw them. In a week's time an individual elk may move throughout only about 2 square miles of its home range. So it's worth hunting out in a circular pattern from spots where you've made recent elk sightings or where you've found fresh elk sign.

By four in the afternoon, elk become more active, perhaps because they're eager to move back to their primary feeding grounds. As elk movement picks up in the evening, your movement should slow down. Once again, the idea is to let the elk come to you. Between 10 PM and 4 AM, elk are enjoying their second most active time of day. Their activity involves moving back to their feeding grounds, and eating on the way.

Contrary to what many hunters believe, this nighttime movement takes place regardless of the lunar phase. So when you can't find elk during the day, don't blame it on the myth that they've been able to feed all night by the light of the moon and are sleeping off their gluttony in some thick patch of timber.

The type of movement that elk hunters most often misread is fright movement. Over the years, elk get accustomed to a variety of noises that cause them to move, but not panic. A man's shout will send elk off for a quarter to a half mile before they settle back down to their normal business of feeding and bedding. The sound of a chain saw has a similar effect. But fire a rifle and they really move out.

So when the season opens and elk are confronted with a barrage of shots, they react much like a ball in a pinball machine, fleeing from one shot only to be sent off in another direction by shots fired from a different location. Elk ricochet around the woods for several days before they settle down to a low-profile routine.

During the first few days of the season, your best strategy is to sit tight in an area that elk would naturally use as a travel lane. Brushy or heavily timbered areas with well-used game trails, corridors of cover in otherwise open areas, and north-slope ridge sides parallel to but below the spine of the divide all offer good possibilities for finding spooked elk on the move.

Once the season is well into its first week, the elk seem to panic less and move with more deliberation. Tracking a spooked elk is often futile considering the distances it may move, especially if you fire a shot at it. But if an elk moves off before a shot is fired, quietly wait for half an hour at the spot where you spooked it before heading out. Taking off in hot pursuit will only make the elk move farther.

Also remember that spooked elk react differently under heavy hunting pressure than they do under light hunting pressure. With light pressure, the elk you frighten may be over the ridge or around the hill, and may move less than a few hundred yards. In the face of heavy pressure, however, the same elk might move five or even ten miles. That's a bit far to tag along behind.

Weather is another factor that often puts elk on the move. These animals are forever shifting locations to take advantage of the most comfortable micro-climates. Cold, heat, wind, snow, rain, humidity, and even cloud cover can influence where elk will move. But more than anything else, weather extremes prompt elk to move to specific locations, where you'll sometimes find them in concentrated numbers.

The combination of cold temperatures and wind is a real moving force; it often sends elk to the lee side of hills and ridges and makes them gather in closed-canopy timber, especially patches that have a good understory to further break the wind. One study on elk's response to cold in the northern Rockies found that the majority of bedding sites were located in clumps of timber on upper slopes, with day beds situated on southern exposures warmed by the sun's heat, while night beds were on northern exposures where timber has a slowing effect on radiant heat loss. These are prime places to hunt elk during times of severe cold.

Extreme weather, whether hot or cold, pushes elk into micro-habitats where they're most comfortable.

Cold without wind may keep elk out in the open on exposed feeding grounds, where they'll move around to feed well after first light. This is when you can really hit the jackpot. Once, after getting a late start on a particularly cold, gray day, I trudged along a border of trees above a long open expanse where elk would often feed. I knew my hunting companions had been back in the trees for over an hour skirting thick timber in search of elk. As I turned up a wood road to join them, I noticed movement through some aspen that made me pause. There below me were nearly fifty elk that had apparently lingered in the open longer than usual to fill their bellies.

Another weather factor of confirmed importance is falling barometric pressure. Elk apparently have been conditioned over generations to go on the move when air pressure drops sharply, and pressure-sensitive parts of their bodies, such as their ears, seem capable of "reading" falling barometric pressure. Elk respond to this condition by moving and feeding more before a storm, which makes them more visible to hunters. These pre-storm periods are especially good times to be hunting in sparse timber where grass and cover are available.

If there is any moral to all this, it's that we should move less when we're hunting elk. Sometimes, as in the early morning, it's best not to move at all. Later in the day, you may want to move very slowly. But as a general rule, let those maddening, meandering elk move to you.

PUNCTURED BULLS

Bull elk may receive as many as fifty puncture wounds from the antlers of other bulls during one rutting season.

Chapter 16

TAKE A STAND

A friend's teenage son had heard some shots and minutes later elk had begun to appear through the trees a quarter of a mile below them. "I know that country really well," my friend recalls, "and I was pretty sure they'd head for this one gully." He and his son ran to the gully's edge and waited. They stayed for about fifteen minutes and nothing happened.

"So we moved on to another point I know and waited there until we got antsy. Then we moved back to the place we had heard the shots. Finally, figuring the elk had moved out of the country, we started back to the truck. Well, there they were, walking through the timber in the gully where we'd first sat. If only we'd stayed there . . . I'm learning slowly but surely that sitting is the way to go."

Hunting elk by sitting on your duff may sound like blasphemy to those dyed-in-the-wool old-timers who preach tracking and stalking, but when it comes to success year after year you might do better by sitting tight. Elk are extremely mobile, rarely bedding down in one spot for more than half an hour, and moving an average of a half mile every few hours. If you're up and moving too, your paths may cross, but chances are good that you'll spook them instead.

Consider their advantages. As herd animals, a group of elk has innumerable eyes, ears, and noses probing the surroundings for danger. Their combined senses are a strong defense. Eyes look in all directions. Noses sniff the subtle currents of the breezes. Ears cup this way and that. Even big bulls are rarely loners; they typically travel in small groups except during rut.

Now consider your disadvantages. As you walk, you attract attention; you step on a stick here, dislodge a rock there. Scent radiates out around you as you travel. You are a waving flag, a blowing whistle. You are something in the wind.

It's easy enough to reverse the situation, though. Just as your mobility gives elk a good chance to detect you, their mobility gives you a good chance to spot them, if you'll just stand still.

Elk are always on the move. They may have a daily home range of one to four miles, and the distance between where they're found one week and the next can easily be two to three miles, even when they aren't migrating. This incessant movement makes sitting in one spot a reasonable hunting option. If you choose a stand wisely, the elk's compulsion for movement will eventually bring the animal(s) within view.

But it's not only elk movement that works to a stationary hunter's advantage, it's *predictable* movement. These very traditional patterns are passed on from generation to generation. Elk use the same summer and winter ranges year after year, as well as the same migration routes to get back and forth between them.

Studies show that the average distance between an elk's centers of activity from year to year may vary by as little as one mile. In some instances it may be even less than that. For example, I know the exact hillside one elk herd will use as part of its winter range each year. The herd regularly appears on that hillside during the

Generation after generation, a herd utilizes traditional summer and winter ranges. Understanding these long-term patterns will put you onto elk more often.

daylight hours just before the close of hunting seasons. And their tracks tell me they use the area at night during the season.

In addition to predictable movement patterns, a fairly open habitat is needed to make stand hunting effective. Look for natural open parks or at least an area where there are open meadows at the edge of extensive timber. (A good mix of forest and parkland is typical of much of the elk habitat in Colorado, southern

Idaho, western Wyoming, and central and southwestern Montana.) The presence of open landscape is necessary to give you a reasonable view of the surroundings. Certainly, elk do a lot of moving through closed timber, but when your view is limited to a few hundred feet, stand hunting is hardly worthwhile. Ideally, you can find a place with a panoramic view of a quarter to half mile, a spot where elk may leave or enter the timber going to and from their feeding grounds. Elk, like cattle, love grass, so they like to eat in the open where the grass grows thickest.

In most cases, a vantage point looking down on open country is preferable to one looking up at it, since your scent is more easily carried uphill even when you're stationary. So pay attention to the wind direction. Keep it in your face if possible.

Also camouflage your silhouette; break it up by keeping trees or rocks or other landforms at your back. Those striking magazine photos of horses, people, or elk standing on a ridgeline are notable because the figures are skylighted. They stand out in contrast to their surroundings, and they're easily identifiable even though they may be far away. You may be standing motionless or even sitting, but you can stick out like a skunk in a chicken house if you don't take a stand in the right place.

Deciding the exact patch of terrain on which to sit is the essence of successful stand hunting, the difference between a dull day on your backside and one that will at least give you a look at some elk.

The crucial question of where to take a stand is dictated to a large extent by the weather. Early in the season, before harsh weather has moved elk around much, you'll have to head for their summer range. That often means getting into the backcountry up near timberline, close to the heads of drainages. If more people hunted these areas at the beginning of the season, the success ratio would definitely rise. But it's hard work to get in there

If you take the proper stand and show patience, the elk may come right to you.

even with a light camp, and harder still to pack an elk out without a horse.

On the other hand, I've scouted such areas in the fall, walking a high divide just above timberline. And in the late afternoon I've seen elk by the dozens appear at the edge of the trees and then step into the lengthening shadows to crop grass out in the open. This has happened not just once, but in drainage head after drainage head.

In hard-to-reach places like this, there isn't much hunting pressure. Consequently, elk come out in the open earlier in the afternoon and stay out later in the morning. Nevertheless, give yourself enough time to scout the surroundings before you blunder into an ill-conceived hunt. Glass the area morning and evening to see where elk leave and enter the trees, then select a vantage point on which to take a stand, remembering that mountain breezes will likely blow downslope in the morning until the sun has a chance to warm the landscape.

As the season progresses and the weather worsens, both hunters and elk are usually persuaded to leave the high country. Hunters inevitably depart first.

Although taking a stand for elk along their traditional migration routes from summer to winter ranges is a possibility, you have to be very lucky with your timing. On their way down from the high country the animals are only going to pass your stand once if it's a true migration. For a few days immediately following a big storm with lots of snow and cold you might take a migration-route stand, but the odds of being at the right place at the right time are really not in your favor.

Instead, hunt the elk's winter range, those exposed hillsides at lower elevations that have a south or southwestern exposure. Once elk have moved out of the high country they start to concentrate around these areas. Unfortunately, hunting pressure at these elevations makes the elk extremely wary, and they tend to hang out in the timber above during the day and move out onto the open slopes to feed only after dark.

A few years ago a mid-season storm brought elk onto a winter range I sometimes hunt. Elk tracks and droppings were all over the open hillside. It seemed like a perfect setup for taking a stand. Tracks clearly indicated where the elk were entering and leaving the timber, so well before daybreak on a number of mornings, several friends and I took stands overlooking the area. Every morning in the dim light of dawn we saw vague forms moving out of the fields and into the timber. The elk passed so close we could hear their hoof falls and breathing, but it was always too dark to distinguish cows from bulls.

Finally, on the fourth morning of waiting, some stragglers stayed in the open until legal hunting hours started. One of them was a bull. A lot of waiting had gone into that payoff, but it had been the only way to effectively hunt these particular elk.

As is the case with many things, the best time to take a stand for elk is when the weather makes you feel most like moving around. When the temperature drops, elk will be moving more and eating more in an attempt to keep warm. This is an especially good time for you to remain in one spot. Get to your stand before daybreak, and stay there until around 9 AM. Unless it's unusually cold, elk will have headed for the timber by this time. Then from around 3 or 4 PM until dark take a stand again.

For the first few days of the season, elk may move around during the middle of the day, but it won't take them long to figure out the situation, and they'll start to timber-up during this time. Heavy hunting pressure can keep them moving about at any time of day though. And this is when patience can work in your favor. Let other hunters get fidgety and do the moving, which in turn will move the elk to you as you sit tight.

When other hunters aren't moving the elk around during the day, use the time to scout. Check for fresh tracks and fresh sign. Find out what stands of timber the elk seem to favor for cover. And then locate a suitable spot to sit and view the open landscape, a spot with the wind in your favor. As in any kind of passive hunting, you'll do your share of sitting and watching shadows and birds and wind in the branches. But suddenly an elk will move out of the trees and then another; they won't know you're there. And you'll suddenly realize that taking a stand for elk makes a lot of sense.

Chapter 17

GO WHERE THE FOOD IS

It's been a decade since Ralph Beer and I hiked the Divide Trail down the backbone of the Gallatin Range in southwestern Montana. That was in late August. For five days we conditioned our legs for hunting season and scouted the terrain for elk.

The trail went like a camel's back for nearly forty miles, up across alpine meadows still flecked with wildflowers and then down into timberline where stunted trees twisted toward the sun. We carefully positioned our camp each night overlooking the head of a drainage: Cliff Creek, Smokey Creek, Big Creek. And every night we got the same tantalizing show.

At first, in the bowl below us there would be only the rich green of the grassy meadow and the glint of silver spring water forming the first headwater trickle of the creek beyond. But as growing shadows nosed across the grass, elk would appear at the forest edge. They'd move silently out of the timber in ones and twos to crop grass as casually as cattle on the open range.

While we sat on the ground watching elk materialize from the trees we picked obsidian chips out of the earth; debris from some Indian arms factory. We were camped where a Native American hunting party had stopped to fashion projectile points while *they* waited for some long-ago elk herd to drift out through the evening shadows and feed on the lush grass. I knew that if snow didn't close me off I'd be back on that divide for the opening of elk season.

Two months later I was there again. I'd found a logging road that got me in close to the divide on the west side. And an hour's worth of hiking beyond the end of the road put me at a spot overlooking a remote east-slope drainage. I smugly made camp there, knowing that by nightfall a big bull would be dressed out in the basin below, and I'd be too tired to do anything but eat fresh elk liver and tumble into my sleeping bag.

"Hunting really shouldn't be this easy," I can remember chuckling to myself.

It wasn't.

By five o'clock that evening, nothing had moved in the meadow below me. And by the close of shooting hours I was still straining to see the first elk move into that open park. The moon came out. The sun came up. Still no elk.

Tired, discouraged, and bewildered, I packed up and hiked off the divide. The elk had moved out. It was that simple. When, where, and why I didn't know. But those meadows had been forsaken for something else. And it certainly wasn't snow that had made them move.

I shot no elk that season, and it wasn't until years later that Terry Lonner, my research biologist friend with the Montana Department of Fish, Wildlife & Parks, supplied some clues to my failure. He's been studying elk habits for over a dozen years. Those habits, especially elk feeding habits, are worth any serious hunter's attention.

According to Terry, elk are considered the beef cow of wild ruminants because of their preference for grass. That's not to say they won't eat anything else; when forced to, they will feed on sagebrush and fir needles and other browse. But they're grazers by nature and love nothing more than getting into a good patch of bluebunch grass or Idaho fescue. That's why their meat tastes closer to beef than any other member of the deer family—one reason why they're such sought-after game.

I'd been aware of this preference for a grass diet when I went after elk in the grassy bowl below the divide. In fact, that's why I went up there. What I didn't know was how particular elk can be—when given the choice—over the way their favorite dish is prepared. It seems they like their grasses rare.

Elk feeding habits are based on getting the most energy-rich food in the most efficient manner possible, Terry told me. This means following the "green up" and keeping ahead of the "brown up." Elk are after new-growth grass that's rich in nutrients. To get this kind of diet, they travel to different parts of their range at different times of year.

Elk often key in on certain species of grass or search out new-growth grass. This knowledge can lead you to the likeliest places for an encounter.

In spring and early summer, elk feed on lower-elevation knobs, knolls, and ridges. They find convex slopes where snow melts first and where grass gets an early start. There is such a place behind my house—a bare knob with a southern slope. It looks like an elk feedlot in April and May. Elk drift out of the timber on late afternoons and feed on the new shoots that have responded to the moisture and warmth that only such an exposure offers at this time of year. However, the grass is as dry and crunchy as granola by midsummer, and the elk have moved up to greener pastures.

By July and August, elk herds have followed the retreating snowline to drainage heads up under the high divides. These concave slopes produce wet meadows where grass stays green long after lower meadows have turned brown. This is the kind of country I'd expected to get an elk in during that unsuccessful season years ago. I had assumed that I'd find elk feeding in the same locations during October as in August, but by October those high, wet bowls have either been hit by snow or frost or have turned rank with moisture and lost much of their new-growth nutrients.

Even in October, though, there are areas where new growth continues. Under sparse forest canopies, where shade has retarded growth, grass may have just recently reached maturity by early fall. It's also protected from frost and, to some extent, snow, and elk congregate here to feed on the most nutritious grass available.

After I'd looked for hour after elkless hour down into that empty drainage head along the Gallatin Range, I'd come to the conclusion that the elk were nowhere near. Had I dropped down into the timber surrounding the bowl, chances are good I would have jumped elk feeding in these protected last-growth areas.

This is not to say elk won't come out into open meadows during the fall. A few years ago, I got into several dozen elk all chowing down in the middle of a ridgeside meadow one early October morning. They bolted before I could collect my startled wits, and I was left with an empty field of brown grass to ponder. Why had they been feeding there when green grass still survived under the trees?

Well, new grass was coming up in the meadow, as I found on closer examination. Early fall moisture combined with a warm Indian summer had spurred a second growth of grass that would be short-lived. But while it lasted, the elk found it a real delicacy. And I found it an excellent place to hunt elk.

But seasonal variations in the locations elk choose to feed have to be coupled with a knowledge of their daily feeding habits if you're going to locate elk consistently. Elk eat roughly a dozen pounds of food daily, a task which research has shown takes about eight hours a day. The other sixteen hours are spent resting and ruminating. It's common knowledge that elk prefer early morning and late afternoon as times to eat. These are prime hours to

Early morning and late evening are usually prime feeding times, but elk feed at night, too. Having success under low-light conditions means knowing where to set up when elk move to and from bedding areas.

still-hunt near good patches of grass. However, elk also love to feed at night, a habit that can push an elk hunter close to tears.

Nighttime seems to provide tangible cover for them, cover that is as real as a thick stand of fir or a tangle of downed lodgepole pine, giving elk a sense of safety even in open areas near roads and houses. Radio tracking of elk has shown that moonlight is not a prerequisite for night feeding. They can find their way to dinner quite well in the dark. Hunting at night, of course, is illegal. But looking for elk at night is not, and it can be a valuable tactic in discovering where to locate elk when you can hunt.

A friend of mine tells the story of waking up early one morning at a high-country hunting camp. Thinking he saw spots in the snow-covered meadow above, he looked through his spotting scope and discovered dozens of elk. Some of them were pawing through the snow to get at the still-fresh regrowth grass below. Others were bedded down and chewing their cuds. All of them were a considerable distance from the nearest cover.

Two hours later, at 4 AM, he awoke again. The elk were still there. So he and his companions decided to make a move, hoping to catch the elk in the open when hunting hours began. After working around through the timber, out of the elks' line of vision, they peered over a rise at the edge of the meadow to see an empty expanse of snow.

Although they'd been given the slip, they did locate where the elk had entered the timber. And by posting themselves nearby, they were able to get an elk later in the season. This tactic of locating feeding elk at night and then posting in nearby timber during the morning and afternoon has proven highly effective.

In addition to seasonal and daily feeding patterns, there are variations brought on by the weather. Snow, of course, will push elk down to lower elevations where feeding is easier. However, even with snow on the ground, they'll be looking for the most nutritious grass available. And during hunting season that continues to be in sparse timber where late growth has occurred and on convex meadows where some regrowth has taken place.

With the advent of a storm, when barometric pressure is falling, it has been my observation that elk get nervous and eat sporadically. They may continue to feed during a light snow, but when the snow gets heavy or the wind comes up, elk head for cover and stay put until the storm passes.

This post-storm period is my favorite time to hunt elk, particularly if the storm has started sometime during the previous day and doesn't let up until the early morning hours. It's a time when elk will feed longer into the daylight hours than usual to fill their empty stomachs. The hunter who knows where the most nutritious elk food is likely to be at that time will have a good chance of intercepting an elk while it's busy satisfying its appetite.

Chapter 18

BEDTIME BULLS

We tend to hunt elk while they're on the move, but the best time to connect with a bull may be while he's in bed. During the rut, an active bull can lose up to 20 percent of his body weight, and he has to regain it if he's to make it through the winter. So after the rut bulls eat and rest more than cows and calves. By 9 or 10 AM a bull has usually bedded down to ruminate, and he'll stay there—getting up at intervals to graze for ten or fifteen minutes—until 3 or 4 PM. So for most of your elk-hunting day, the animals are in or around their beds.

Generally, bulls pick higher, more rugged terrain than cows and calves, which find security in numbers. Bulls bed down in ones and twos, and have to rely on their surroundings, so they look for heavy cover, rough country, and remoteness.

The weather plays a big role. When it's cold and sunny, bulls prefer to lie in the open and soak up the rays. Since they want cover close by, small openings in timber on southern slopes and terraces on steep hillsides are likely spots. But when wind comes up, bulls seek cover, not only to get out of the draft, but because wind noise interferes with their hearing. They'll head for the thickest cover they can find, which is usually on northern slopes.

The bed itself is still the best indicator of a bull's whereabouts and what he's doing. Locating beds is easiest when there's snow on the ground, but they're also discernible in mud, dry soil, and ground litter like pine needles. Research suggests that if the urine mark in the bed is in the middle, it's a bull; at the edge, a cow. This method is thought to be roughly 80-percent reliable, since the anatomy of the animal determines where the stream lands.

Bulls like to bed down in ones and twos, preferably in rugged country with a wide field of view.

There are other indicators as well. If you find a bed by itself, or with only two or three others nearby, it's probably a bull's. Look for the tracks of antlers in the dirt or snow. These grooves are cut by the antler tines when the animal tilts his head to stretch or scratch.

Aging a bed is an inexact science at best. Generally, it's a matter of determining whether a bed is fresh (meaning minutes to hours) or old (half a day to many days or weeks). Check the hardness of the bed; see if the urine is frozen and, unappealing as it may be, check the urine for scent. If it still smells strong, the bed may be only a few hours old.

The tracks that lead away from the bed tell you what to do next. If they're evenly spaced, a foot and a half to two feet apart, the elk has moved off unhurriedly. But if they're in widely spaced sets of four, the elk bounded out of bed, probably spooked by you.

When you find even tracks, follow them carefully, but if they're frantic, wait at least a half hour before taking up the trail. Watch the tracks as you move along. They will eventually change from a run to a rapid, direct walk to a meandering pattern that shows he no longer thinks he's in danger and is looking for a place to bed down again. When this happens, follow very cautiously.

Bulls tend to use the same bedding areas year after year, and once you have them located, there are two ways to hunt them. The first is to still-hunt very slowly and quietly, though in my experience over half the bulls caught in their beds spook before you get a shot at them. At least you'll have fresh tracks to follow.

The other method is to take a stand at one of these areas at dawn and dusk when the elk are likely to be returning to or leaving their beds. The stand should be within a few hundred yards

Approaching close enough to get a good shot at a bull on its bed can be tricky.

of the bedding area and along the most likely route to feeding grounds.

Last fall, for instance, I found an unobtrusive ridge back in the timber within a quarter-mile of an open, grassy saddle. The ridge was strewn with deadfalls and dotted with bull beds. It's a difficult spot to still-hunt, so next fall I know right where I'll put a stand. Because one of the best ways to get a bull is to get into his bedroom.

Elk Hunter's Diary

A large, majestic bull elk checks his back trail. (Ted Rose)

Bulls thrash saplings as part of their preparations for the rut. (Ted Rose)

An aggressive elk can shred nearly all the bark off a good-sized tree, leaving a signpost for other elk and a valuable clue for hunters. (Ted Rose)

Colorado gives up more elk each year than any other state. (Fiduccia Enterprises)

Every hunter thrills to the sound of a bugling elk in early fall. (Ted Rose)

Solitary bulls may remain in the high country despite heavy snow cover. (Ted Rose)

One more step and this nice bull will present the perfect shot opportunity. (Ted Rose)

A little snow on the ground makes tracking much easier. If you're careful and patient a trophy like this could be your reward. (Fiduccia Enterprises)

When the gun season opens, the wide availability of forage often means that elk are spread out and higher up in the mountains. Hunters must work harder to find them. (Fiduccia Enterprises)

It isn't easy to get close to a cagey old bull on the alert. (Ted Rose)

This is a welcome sight for any hunter after a long day afield. (Ted Rose)

BUGLES AND BACHELORS

A bull elk that has already collected a harem is less likely to respond to a hunter's bugle than a bachelor bull, since by challenging another bull he might lose his harem. Unfortunately, these harem bulls are more apt to be the trophies.

A cow elk tends to choose a trophy bull as a mating partner because a bull's large, symmetrical antlers are a visible sign of a healthy, forage-savvy male who has mastered the subtleties of adapting successfully to the local environment.

Chapter 19

THE RUT

The sound many people associate with fall in the Rocky Mountain West is a very weird sound indeed. It's an almost comical cross between a high-pitched squeal and a grunt-like roar. Someone with a sense of humor or a tin ear dubbed the sound that bull elk make "bugling." When bull elk start bugling at the end of August each year, the sound signals the start of rut. And the breeding season, as practiced by bull elk, is a very raucous affair.

Triggered by the decreasing number of hours of light in a day, a bull elk's hormones kick into overdrive during rut. His bugle is a form of self-aggrandizement, an advertisement of his sexual prowess for the benefit of cow elk and a warning to other bulls to steer clear or face a fight.

Along with bugling, the bull thrashes bushes and saplings with his antlers to show that he's ready to take on any rivals and as a way to spread his personal scent for females to whiff. Not content to leave it at that, the bull urinates on himself to produce a kind of raunchy, animal Old Spice that female elk find attractive. He also makes wallows where he pees in damp earth, stirs up the mixture with his hooves and antlers, and rolls in the resulting rank mud. He then smears his mud- and urine-caked hair on bushes and trees to leave his love scent for females.

The more dominant, mature, and confident the bull, the more he does this disgusting stuff and the more he bugles. The bugle starts with a high-pitched squeal that may rise several octaves and then end with a series of low-pitched, resonant grunts. The high-pitched squeal carries long distances to attract new females to the bull's harem. The low-pitched grunt doesn't carry well but acts as a macho, reassuring sound to the cows that the bull has already attracted and is attempting to keep nearby. If a harem cow starts to wander off, the herd bull runs after her and cuts her off, even using his antlers to prod her back into place.

Eating little and drinking frequently, a harem-tending bull has his work cut out for him during the typical month-long rut.

In his book *Elk Country*, Dr. Valerius Geist sums up the mature bull's role during mating season: "A bull's aim, clearly, must be to breed as many females as possible. The earlier he begins advertising, the more females he can 'convince' of his ability to provide effective shelter from harassment from young bulls, while teaching the cows that they are 'in control.' The more he advertises, the fewer females are likely to leave him, attracted and made curious about other actively bugling bulls. Consequently, the frequency of bugling coincides with the greatest amount of female activity (morning and evening). Also, it is in the bull's interest to out-advertise other bulls or to shut them up if it is in his power to do so. Thus, an advertising rival who happens to be nearby will be sought out and aggressively silenced. That's why bugling attracts bulls."

And that's why many early-season hunters—mainly archers and muzzleloaders—imitate the sound of bulls bugling: to attract wild-eyed, rank-smelling bulls close enough to kill with an arrow or rifle ball. The trick, of course, is to be able to make the strange vocalizations of both bull and cow elk. Old-timers used to mimic

There's nothing more exciting than bugling in a large bull. (Jay Cassell)

Most archery seasons coincide with the rut, giving bowhunters a chance to bring elk in close enough to loose an arrow.

elk with their own vocal chords (ouch!) or by blowing into a plastic pipe or copper tube plugged at the end and notched to make a giant whistle. But the most effective modern elk call is a diaphragm that you put in your mouth and tune with the pressure of your tongue. Used with a grunt tube to add resonance and distance to the call, mouth diaphragms are very effective. But God help the hunter with a quick gag reflex. Another option is a reed or diaphragm that's put into a mouthpiece and then blown.

Getting a sound that's convincing to elk out of any elk call is a matter of practice, practice, and more practice, and it's not something I can talk you through in the pages of this book. To learn various elk calls, including the high-pitched whistle of a cow, the single-note squeal of a bull, and the full-blown bull bugle, you need to hear elk, or a good caller, produce the sounds. There are a number of tapes and videos on the market that will teach you the right sounds and when to make them. For online shopping, try

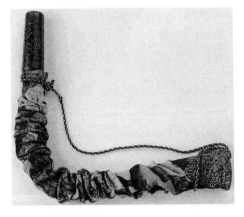
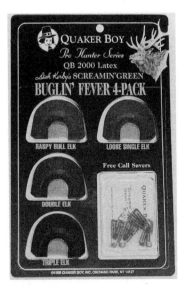

Grunt tubes and diaphragms, like these from Quaker Boy Game Calls, are the most common types of calls for bugling.

http://www.allpredatorcalls.com, http://www.backcountryinc.com, http://www.outdoorsuperstore.com, and http://www.cabelas.com. When your cassette and elk call arrive, start practicing.

The true test of how good you are as an elk caller comes in the field when you're actually trying to lure in an elk. First, you'll have to locate a bull. In forested areas interspersed with open meadows, like Colorado's aspen-covered high country, you may be able to locate elk by scouting with binoculars or a spotting scope. If you see only cows, know that bulls won't be far away when the rut is on. In more heavily forested areas, you may have to troll for bulls by bugling as you move through the timber. Walk at a moderate pace where you think elk should be, bugle about every quarter of a mile, and listen for a reply.

Once you see or hear a bull, the fun begins. There's nothing that can get your adrenalin flowing faster than bringing a bull to within twenty or thirty yards.

There are some tricks, of course:

- Big bulls tend to make a fuller-sounding squeal with a more resonant grunt than smaller bulls, but bugle quality is not always an indicator of size. Some very puny bugles come packaged in very large bulls and visa versa. So call in any bull you can until you have a chance to see him. Then decide if he's the bull of your dreams.

- When you're trying to get a bull to respond, use your big, hairy, harem bull call with a multi-octave squeal and a deep, resonant grunt. If you get a response, continue your harem bull call after a short delay. If that doesn't work try imitating the call of the bull you're trying to pull in.

- As the bull gets closer, switch to a cow whistle in order to give the bull the sense that he's coming in on a harem bull's females. And, remember, as the bull closes in he may bugle very little or not at all.

- Before the bull you're calling gets too close, you need to set yourself up for a clear shot of not more than twenty to thirty yards with a bow. You'll want to be hidden or camouflaged behind trees or brush with several shot lanes to choose from in the direction the bull is approaching. Ideally, you'll be at approximately the same elevation as the bull. And you'll need the wind in your face or the bull will scent you and be gone.

- In order to get the bull close enough for a decent shot, "throw" your call away from your location by pointing the end of your calling tube behind you. You want the bull to think the call is coming from farther away so he'll keep moving closer.

When you call a bull in for the first time and then draw back your bowstring and wait for him to make the last few critical steps, you'll be a confirmed bugle hunter even before you let the arrow fly.

Chapter 20

POST RUT

Scouting for elk is a preseason pastime guaranteed to bolster the hopes of the most accomplished hunter. It's an experience that laughs in the face of the ridiculously low elk hunter success rate which, in my home state of Montana, is under 20 percent. Scouting for elk has all sorts of positive influences on hunting plans and on hunters' psyches. But it fails to answer one basic question: Why do you see so many big bulls before the regular rifle season opens and so few after it begins?

Big bulls are something of a breed unto themselves. They operate a bit differently than cows, calves, spikes, and raghorns. During the summer, a mature bull's main concern is food. He has to stock up on the most nutritious forage he can find before rut begins because he relies on stored body fat to carry him through a time when he will eat very little. To maximize his summertime energy gain, a bull compromises a certain amount of security. He moves out of the trees into open bowls at the heads of drainages where grasses are rich and thick. And he frequents expansive natural grassland parks in the rolling highlands. It's in these locations that you see bulls, even during the day, when you're traveling those ridgeline gravel roads on weekend camping trips or when you hike into a timberline lake to fish for cutthroats in the middle of August.

It's the bull's single-minded push for food that makes him so visible during the summer. And it's a preoccupation that can be a life or death concern, since the more fat a bull retains after the rigors of rut, the greater his chances of surviving the demands of winter.

Once the rut is underway—in September and early October—a bull's attention turns from gathering food to gathering cows. In his lust for a harem, he's noisy and showy. You can hear his distinctive bugling; you can see where he has torn up the ground with his hooves and where he has thrashed saplings with his antlers. And he's on the move more than at any other time of year. His movements, his noisiness, and his rutting displays make him a conspicuous creature.

If you're an archer, you know where the bulls are during the rut, even if you can't get close enough for an effective arrow shot. If you're a rifle hunter, you count the days until the opening of the season because you're convinced you know where you'll find a trophy.

Finally, the rut is over, the rifle season begins, and the big bulls disappear. It may not always be quite that clear-cut, but it usually seems that way. Part of the disappearing act has to do with the social grouping of any elk herd. Except during the rut, mature bulls tend to be solitary creatures. Occasionally, they run in stag groups, but more often they're by themselves. Their solitary nature doesn't develop, however, until bulls are about three and a half years old. Juvenile bulls—spikes and raghorns—very often stay with the cows and calves.

This latter group is most noticeable after the rut simply because there is a lot more movement to be seen in numbers. A lone bull, even when he's walking through the woods, is more

After the rut the biggest bulls seem to disappear. (Jay Cassell)

difficult to spot. The bull's reclusive nature is not pure happenstance. It's probably evolution's way of avoiding competition for food between bulls and cows with their calves.

Being alone, especially after the rut, is a way for bulls to avoid being easily detected by predators, including hunters. The animals are worn out from the efforts of rut and from eating little or nothing during that period. Older bulls are particularly stressed at this time; they lose more fat reserves than younger bulls and are therefore more vulnerable to predation and to the punishment of winter weather.

The animals' response to all this is to find islands of habitat that still offer nutritious food in the form of dried grasses, forbs, and seed heads—forage rich in protein that can offer high-energy intake. These islands of forage are the key to finding bulls after the rut. It's appropriate to think of them as islands because they tend to be small, isolated patches of food encompassed by habitat that has little value to a hungry elk. It may be a grassy knoll or a small opening surrounded by thick trees. It may be a windswept ridge or the mouth of a ravine or a path of hillside grass between the forest and the lowlands.

Isolated, however, doesn't have to mean remote. Bulls don't necessarily work different country than cows, calves, and spikes. They may be nearby, but still aloof.

Not many years ago I was hunting along an 8,000-foot divide that I'd never hunted before. I'd been working toward a sparsely forested saddle that looked as if it would provide elk forage as well as easy access for elk to travel from one drainage to another. Wanting to approach the saddle from above, I had almost worked my way to the top of an adjacent knob through eight inches of snow when I jumped a six-point bull that nearly kicked snow in my face as he disappeared down the hill.

What at first appeared to be an unlikely place for an elk proved to be an ideal micro-habitat for a lone bull. On the west side of the knob was a clearing about the size of a modest house. It was big enough to grow a good crop of grass during the summer, but still small enough to keep from filling up with snow in the winter. Around the edges of the clearing the bull had easily gotten to the grass with little sign of effort. Following his tracks down the steep east side of the divide, I came to his bed perched on a small terrace in the middle of thick lodgepole pine.

Not a quarter of a mile away—on the slopes of the saddle I'd been heading for—thirty to forty cows and calves and a couple of spikes mingled through the sparse trees. The place the bull had chosen and the place the cows with their calves had chosen are typical of where you're likely to find both at this time of year. The bull was in rougher country; it was steeper, rockier, and had more snow despite an elevation difference of only a few hundred feet. Although it was an area a large bull—even a tired one—could live and feed in quite comfortably, it wasn't a spot that cows and calves, which need larger continuous areas of forage, would handle easily.

These islands of forage are what you should scout for before the elk season opens, since where you see the bulls during the preseason says little about where they'll go after the rut. Look not only for pockets of grasses and forbs, but try to imagine what those areas will be like when snow is on the ground. Will they be drifted in or blown clear? Will the sun melt them off? Will nearby trees minimize snow accumulations?

The question of snow conditions is important because elk, particularly bulls, are trying to maximize their energy intake and minimize their energy output after the rut. An area may be rich in forage, but if that forage is buried under several feet of snow a bull is going to have to expend too much energy getting at it to make it worthwhile.

The general elevations at which bulls seek islands of forage will be largely dependent upon the overall snow conditions in a region. Obviously, if little snow has fallen in the high country, there is no reason for the elk to seek lower elevations. On the other hand, heavy snows can force bulls to move to pockets of forage on the periphery of winter ranges where cows and calves may have already gathered.

But heavy snow in the high country is not always a sure sign that bulls will move down, as a recent midseason stop at a game-check station revealed. In Montana, hunters are required to stop at check stations set up along access roads whether or not they've had a successful hunt. Fish and game personnel gather information on hunter numbers, where they've hunted, and what game they've seen, in addition to hunter success and the sex, age, weight, and condition of game taken.

I had stopped at the check station out of curiosity more than anything else. It was in an area I was unfamiliar with, and I wanted to ask some questions about the hunting conditions. Besides, there was a big bull hanging from the scales as I approached. I got out of the car just in time to hear the checker ask where the hunter had gotten the bull. The hunter, a middle-aged man with a ruddy face, shook his head with a resigned grin and jerked his thumb toward the sky: "Right up on top."

Right up on top in that part of the country was at 9,000 feet. It's an area interspersed with large open parks and heavy timber. And the snow up there had to be at least three feet deep. It seemed like a very inhospitable spot for a bull to be hanging out.

After the hunter and his party had left, I asked the fish and game man where most of the large bulls were being taken. "Like the man said," he answered with a laugh, "right up on top. Right now they're up high feeding on south slopes at night and getting onto north slopes that are real jungles in the daytime."

In fact, what the bulls had found—in a place most of us would consider impossible for an elk, let alone a hunter—was a fairly ideal living arrangement. Even at those high elevations, they had found very good feeding conditions: windswept ridges where the ground was completely bare and where dried grasses and forbs lay exposed for easy eating.

There is little competition for food in these areas because of the relatively small number of bulls occupying the habitat. In addition, these islands of forage are surrounded by snow conditions that predators find difficult to traverse. So all a bull has to do is get out of the wind to maintain his energy balance. He can bed down on the lee side of a ridge in deep snow where there is plenty

Solitary bulls often hold out in islands of high cover despite the presence of deep snow.

of insulation. In some places, bulls spend the entire winter in these isolated pockets of habitat.

Of course, one of the main reasons the bulls select these high elevations is hunting pressure, which, after weather, is the number one influence on where elk move and where they want to stay. The more horse hunters using an area, the higher the elk are going to be. The hunter on a horse can handle deeper snow and travel greater distances than the foot hunter. When present in any numbers, these hunters push elk higher in search of security.

But the underlying factor in finding big bulls after rut still remains those isolated patches of food. In an area where I regularly hunt elk there's a draw that opens up at the bottom into a gentle slope of sage and grass. The top of the draw—a quarter mile and several hundred feet higher—gives way to an exposed knoll also covered with grass and sagebrush. The south slope of the draw has stands of old fir and little understory vegetation that would interest an elk. On the north slope, lodgepole is so thick that nothing much sprouts on the forest floor except moss. There is, however, one spot where a patch of beetle-killed trees was blown down eight or nine years ago. The small clearing has sprouted a good crop of grass in the years since it opened up, even though it gets little sun.

Although the larger openings at the top and bottom of the draw have often attracted cows and calves during the hunting season, I was more interested in the little clearing surrounded by thick timber. A few years ago, I made a point of swinging by that opening every time I went hunting in the area. It was a long shot, of course, and I didn't pin my hopes of getting a bull on that one single spot. I made the rounds of a whole string of isolated pockets. On the last day of the season that year, I approached that island of grass through a thick stand of pine, and my view down a narrow hallway of trees ended with a five-point bull.

CHRONIC WASTING DISEASE

Chronic wasting disease (CWD), first discovered in the wild in 1981, is a fatal disease of the central nervous system that affects whitetails, mule deer, and elk, causing sponge-like holes in their brain and spinal cord. CWD has been found in Colorado, Wyoming, South Dakota, New Mexico, Nebraska, and Wisconsin. These states, in addition to some neighboring but currently unaffected states, like Montana, are conducting ongoing surveillance to track and limit the spread of the disease. In addition, research continues into the cause of the disease and its possible effect on humans. The Federal Centers for Disease Control and Prevention have found no evidence that CWD is transmissible to humans.

However, elk and deer hunters are advised to avoid shooting animals that look sick. Symptoms of CWD include listlessness, emaciation, and salivation. Deer and elk with the disease may stand with legs splayed and head lowered. If you see an animal with these symptoms, report its location to the local fish and game department.

Hunters in areas known to have animals infected with CWD should take the following precautions with the game they kill:

- Wear rubber gloves when field dressing game.

- Avoid making contact with brain and spinal cord tissue.

- Bone meat from the carcass and cut off all fatty tissue.

- Discard brain, spinal cord, eyes, spleen, and lymph nodes.

Continued on next page

- Thoroughly wash meat knives and saws after use.

- If a commercial operator processes the meat, request that it be kept separate from the meat of other animals.

Each state where CWD occurs has different regulations pertaining to the disease and different requirements for hunters. Check the fish and game website of the state where you will be hunting to obtain the specifics. For current information on all aspects of CWD, visit the Chronic Wasting Disease Alliance website at http://www.cwd-info.org.

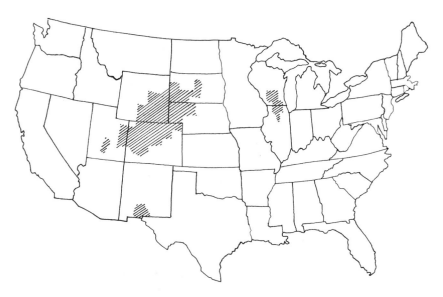

Chronic wasting disease in wild elk and deer.

Chapter 21

MAKING THE MOST OF COLD WEATHER

Elk season along the Continental Divide is a time of changes. Opening day may arrive as balmy as a summer breeze, and as you walk draws and ridges looking for fresh elk sign you may spot songbirds that show little interest in heading south. But the season evolves, and one day you awake to a hard wind that blows all the way to dusk. Snow starts falling during the night and continues throughout the next day, and somewhere in the condensed darkness of the following night the stars snap on and cold settles like a stone.

Stepping into a day on which the temperature has tumbled to the basement fine tunes my hunting skills faster than anything else I know. Three of the five elk I've shot over the last five years were taken when the temperature was in the teens or below. I'd go so far as to say that I got those elk because of the cold.

Elk do things when the temperature drops below 20 degrees that they don't do when it's warmer. Perhaps even more than snow, cold weather prompts elk to move to lower elevations. Frigid temperatures also affect what side of a ridge elk bed down on, what type of cover they seek, and how and when they feed and move. The hunter who is aware of the influence of cold weather on elk behavior stands a better-than-average chance of finding animals when the temperature drops into the teens or even below zero.

Traditional hunting lore has it that snow is the prime catalyst in getting elk to move from their high summer range down to where they are easier to hunt. Snow certainly has its effects, but research on elk movement indicates that they can easily walk through snow that's a foot and a half deep before the going gets rough, and a big bull may be unhampered by up to two or even three feet of snow, depending on its consistency.

Once it gets cold in the high country, though, things begin to happen. The open alpine meadows and the spare timberline forests provide no protection from the effects of radiant cooling at night, and body heat just dissipates out into the clear, unobstructed skies. In these conditions, elk start to head lower in search of thicker forest cover and elevations less exposed to the influence of wind and its additional chilling effects. Even in the absence of snow, severe cold may spur elk into fall migration routes. Cold and snow provide a double whammy that brings elk within even closer reach.

So the first real cold snap—when temperatures hit the low teens—is a good time to look for elk along traditional migration corridors. Fall storms that come in for a day or two and are immediately followed by a sudden and deep drop in temperature under clear skies provide ideal hunting conditions. But get out there on the migration travel lanes even if the cold isn't preceded by snow.

As the elk descend from the high country in the face of really cold weather, they'll be looking for several things to satisfy their needs. They'll want to find a source of nutritious food to fire their heat-producing body furnaces, since calories equal BTUs as

Snow and seriously cold temperatures signal the best time to stake out a spot along traditional elk migration corridors.

much for elk as they do for humans. And once elk have found a good source of food, they'll want to conserve the body heat it produces by finding a place to hide and bed that minimizes heat loss.

But cold-weather feeding sites and cold-weather bedding sites aren't always close together. And since low temperatures prompt elk to feed more in order to stay warm, the animals will be going back and forth between feeding and bedding sites more frequently than usual. This increased movement makes them more visible to hunters.

The best bedding sites under cold conditions are found in conifer forests that have thick canopies. These can usually be found on north slopes, where optimum shade and moisture produce dense timber stands. The umbrella formed by the tree branches holds in a certain amount of heat, preventing it from radiating quickly into the atmosphere. Clouds can have the same effect, but when it gets really cold the skies are usually very clear.

Setting out on the last day of elk season some years ago, I moved under stars that glittered so sharply I could almost feel their edges. I left behind a house with frozen water pipes and a wife who agreed that they could remain that way because I had only one more chance to put elk steaks on the table for the winter.

My toes and fingers ached even though I walked quickly up a Forest Service fire break that had been cut through thick timber years earlier. The break seemed my best bet for covering ground through otherwise tough terrain. As I walked, I peered under the tight cover of fir branches looking for bedded elk.

As I approached the crest of the north slope and the end of the fire break, I slowed my pace to a real still-hunting crawl. At the end of the tunnel the fire break made through the trees, I could see that the sun had just begun to hit the south slope on the opposite side of the ridge. I was standing, letting my eyes re-adjust to the darkness beneath the trees, when I heard the sound and noticed the legs. The elk had given a grunt of exertion when it got up from its bed, and suddenly it was standing there like a present.

More than likely, it was the clear, cold skies that gave the bull to me. I later concluded from his tracks that the elk had spent much of the previous frigid day feeding and basking in the sun on the open south slope less than a hundred yards from his bed. Then he'd entered the timber on the fire break and stepped into a dense knot of conifers to stay as warm as possible for the night. I suspect he, too, had seen the morning sun hit the south slope and was getting up to seek its warmth.

That elk had found an ideal situation, given the cold weather. The thick timber needed for a warm bedding site and the open slopes needed for grass were very close together at this spot. In fact, any east-west ridgeline will provide both a north and south aspect within very close proximity to one another. These are ideal places in which to hunt when it's cold. In the face of light hunting pressure, elk feed and sun in the open during the day and head for the relative warmth of thick timber only after the sun goes down. This is just the reverse of what they usually do, and an elk hunter who knows this has a distinct advantage.

It's sometimes difficult, however, for elk to find a place that offers ideal bedding and feeding conditions as well as light hunting pressure. So elk need additional bedding and feeding sites.

When cold weather is combined with snow cover, elk use the insulative qualities of snow to keep themselves warm. It seems ironic, but where snow cover is patchy, remaining only in shaded draws or in drifts on windward bits of terrain, elk will actually seek it out for a bedding spot during cold spells. For this reason, snow pockets are well worth checking, particularly at daybreak.

Deep snow, on the other hand, produces what are called "tree wells" around the bases of lone, large conifers. Low-hanging branches keep snow from piling up under the tree while snow depths around the periphery may accumulate to the height of the lowest limbs. The "well" produced beneath the tree offers almost complete protection from wind, and the mass of the tree trunk retains enough heat to attract elk in cold weather. In some areas of the northern Rockies, elk have actually been observed competing for such prime bedding sites in extremely cold weather. So it's worth scouting for big, live conifers that can produce such tree wells.

As for feeding grounds, elk may want to stay very close to cover when hunting pressure is great. This is when secluded natural openings surrounded by timber become cold-weather gathering points for hungry elk. They can feed on the grasses but never be more than a few dozen yards from cover.

In areas where you aren't immediately aware of the lay of the land, a 7.5-minute series topographic map will indicate the locations of such natural openings. And don't overlook small clearcuts as possible cold-weather feeding grounds.

On the other extreme, elk may move a mile or more out of the timber onto completely open terrain where the openness itself provides some security. A herd of elk feeding in open country is difficult to sneak up on because your presence can usually be detected by at least one elk, who will then warn the others of danger. If you find a concentration of elk in the open during the day

Elk occasionally move far out into open terrain, making it extremely difficult for you to approach unnoticed.

in a cold snap, it's best to locate where they've been coming out of the timber and wait for them there.

Even if other hunters make plays on such exposed elk, you're better off waiting for them near the timber. I once spent several hours watching sixty elk—some big bulls among them—as they milled and circled over a square mile of rolling hayfields below me. I could see three hunters trying to get close to the elk from three different directions, but even though shots were fired, not an elk went down. Finally, harassed enough, the herd headed uphill in my direction, and I was able to select a nice bull as the elk entered the timber in the same tracks they'd made that morning.

The typical cold-weather elk behavior I've been describing can be curtailed by two accompanying weather conditions that occasionally occur when the temperature drops. Wind has a real effect on elk when it's cold. They'll do almost anything to avoid it, usually forsaking food in favor of finding a calm pocket in the surrounding terrain. Look for these pockets when it's cold and windy, and you'll probably fill your elk tag.

Temperature inversions are less frequent but also worthy of note. Occasionally, weather conditions force a wedge of warm air up over a wedge of cold air, trapping the cold air close to the ground. The temperature difference between these layers of air can be dramatic, as much as 20 degrees, so this phenomenon really can influence elk whereabouts. Coming down out of the timber toward lower, open feeding grounds, elk may run into the trapped cold air, turn around, and go back uphill where it's warmer.

I once spent a cold morning unsuccessfully using my tried-and-true-cold-weather hunting tactics for elk—checking lower timber edges, south slopes, and open hayfields. Around noon, a friend of mine who'd decided to hunt higher caught up with me in a sweat. He told me that only two hundred feet higher on the ridge the temperature was near 30 degrees. I'd been hunting in single-digit temperatures. Later, we caught up with a herd of elk lounging in comfort on the grassy south side of a high ridge.

Perhaps the most important thing to remember about hunting elk in the cold is that their behavior at this time consists of a delicate balancing act. Elk have to move and eat to keep warm, but they also have to stay still to conserve energy. Your awareness of how they maintain this balance is the key to successful elk hunting in cold weather.

Chapter 22

THE LAW OF LEAST EFFORT

In an attempt to minimize their energy expenditures, elk tend to follow what is called "the law of least effort." This is especially true in the fall, when they are trying to maximize the fat reserves that will carry them through the winter. For example, under the law of least effort, elk react to snow cover in very specific ways. They feed where snow depths are scantiest, in such spots as windswept ridges, sunny south slopes, and below forest canopies. When traveling through snow, they choose routes where the snow is softest, avoiding windslab and sun-crusted snow that make walking difficult. When groups of elk move through snow, they walk single file, beating down a path to make traveling easier for most of the herd members.

When using the law of least effort, elk may even switch from browsing on grass to foraging on bushes in order to avoid exerting the energy required to paw through snow for food.

An elk's choice of bedding sites also may reflect this law. To minimize heat loss—and consequently the need for energy expenditure—elk often bed under dense forest cover that acts as a thermal blanket. Dense ridgeline cover at the top of north slopes makes a particularly attractive elk bedding site because little energy is needed to walk over to the south side of the ridge. During the day, elk can feed on grass exposed by melting snow and also take advantage of solar heat gain offered by the open southern aspect.

Elk prefer to feed in areas where forage density is greatest because it minimizes the amount of moving they have to do to fill their stomachs. This, no doubt, is why elk like haystacks. But in a natural setting they often gather in moist areas where grass and shrub growth is greater than on the surrounding dry land. Elk also tend to feed in groups to minimize the time each individual must spend watching for danger and to maximize feeding time. The more open the country, the larger the group is likely to be.

Employing the law of least effort when spooked, elk often make their initial getaway moves in a downhill direction, following a route containing few obstacles. Gravity assists in putting

Smart hunters know how to take advantage of an elk's propensity to minimize the effort necessary to feed, bed, or escape danger. (Jay Cassell)

If this young bull spooks, he'll most likely take the fastest route to put distance between himself and danger before turning in the direction he ultimately wants to go.

some quick distance between them and the potential danger. Later on, they may move uphill again at a slower pace.

I've seen groups and individual elk use this least-effort maneuver to elude hunters. Perhaps the largest bull I ever came close to shooting eyed me for half a second from the other side of a nearby rock outcropping before disappearing. We were so close that within seconds, I was at the rocks looking uphill for a shot. Rocks sliding in the canyon below alerted me to the bull's downward departure. I'd been heartily outsmarted by the law of least effort.

Although the law worked in a very specific way to assist in that bull's survival, it also works in a much broader way in an elk herd's use of its traditional home range. By staying on the same block of terrain year after year, the herd learns how to utilize the landscape while expending a minimum amount of energy. The group doesn't waste its strength looking for the good pockets of food or the best windbreak in the face of a winter storm; it already knows where such spots are.

Elk employ the law of least effort in a general pattern of behavior as well as in response to specific situations. It's a natural law elk hunters should always keep in mind.

Chapter 23

TOUGH HUNTING FOR EASIER ELK

A writer for *Time* once wrote that elk hunting "is about as pop-ular in Montana as golf is in Palm Springs, California." Frankly, as a thirty-five-year transplant to elk country, I find elk hunting easier than golf. Someone new to chasing elk might vote for running after a little white ball and yelling "fore." But elk hunters yell four letter words, too.

Still, if I were learning to hunt elk from scratch, I'd want some-one to tell me about the ironies of the pursuit. And I guess the biggest irony of hunting elk is the one that concludes: the tougher you make the hunt, the easier it'll be to get an elk. The truth of this irony lies in the elks' ability to predict hunter patterns. Native Americans were wise to this, and we might take a cue from them.

When the Indians found hunting success slipping it was usually because they'd hunted an area so often that the elk could predict their hunting patterns and had moved off to undisturbed areas. The Indian answer to the problem was to consult a shaman, who would heat an elk shoulder bone until it cracked and showed him the way to better hunting grounds. Elk-hunting success invariably rose for awhile in this new area because the animals weren't used to having hunters around and hadn't had time to figure out their patterns.

It's not quite so easy for the modern elk hunter because any good hunting area that's within easy reach of roads is usually packed with hunters. However, following the shaman's advice we can move into more remote areas and actually find elk hunting easier. Elk behave differently near traveled roads than they do near closed roads or where there are no roads at all. Studies show that it takes elk approximately forty-eight hours to acclimate to the opening of hunting season, with its accompanying disturbance, and to shift into their security-is-foremost behavior.

Their two basic reactions to hunting pressure are to use heavily hunted areas in ways that optimize their security (and minimize hunter success) or to depart for relatively undisturbed areas and lead a normal life. The elk that remain within easy road access prefer thick timber and pole stands, spending most of their time on north slopes where cover is typically the densest. Those in unroaded areas gravitate toward open timber where grass grows in the understory, spending a lot of time on open south slopes in addition to north slopes.

During hunting season, elk in roaded areas generally spend a great deal more time in dense conifers and much less time in open areas than they normally would. On the other hand, elk in unroaded areas seem little affected by the presence of hunters without vehicles.

Basically, once elk are away from the predictable areas of high hunting pressure, they become easier to hunt. They spend more time out in the open. They frequent a greater diversity of places. They move about more during the day. And they spook less easily.

There's one other advantage to making things tough on yourself: There are more bulls back there away from the cars and

You'll rarely see a sight like this near a roaded area during hunting season.

the trucks and the hordes of other hunters. And the bulls have bigger antlers.

Bulls seem to respond more to hunting pressure than cows do. They move out of heavily hunted areas faster than cows, and those that don't move out don't get to grow very big. Recent research in Idaho revealed some interesting findings. Bulls in heavily roaded areas didn't live past five and a half years and only 5 percent lived to maturity. Where roads were closed to motorized traffic, some of the bulls survived seven and a half years and 16 percent of them lived to maturity. In unroaded country, a number of bulls lived for more than ten years and over 30 percent of the bull population consisted of mature animals, according to the report.

Let's consider what "tough hunting" means. Don't panic. There are different degrees of tough. Getting away from motorized traffic doesn't have to mean going roadless. An increasing number of old logging roads have served their original purpose and have been closed to all motorized traffic. In effect, these roads become "super trails" that you can follow on foot into easier hunting country. The tough part comes with the distance you have to hike in to get to good hunting and then the distance you must pack out your elk.

Traffic on heavily used logging roads may push elk several miles. It can move them into the next drainage or even beyond that drainage if a road traverses the ridgeline. Usually, however, you can figure on one mile from an open road as the point beyond which elk begin to settle down and make hunting easier for you.

Topography has a lot to do with how far elk move. Where hills and ridges act as a sight and sound barrier between elk and vehicles, the distance they have to move to feel secure may be as little as half a mile if dense forest covers the terrain. Ridgetop roads and roads through bowl-shaped basins are the most disruptive. Where these occur you may have to walk several miles to get to easier hunting.

While closed roads offer the easiest foot access to undisturbed hunting grounds, trails may provide another, albeit sometimes tougher, alternative. Trails are usually steeper than roads, but they may be more direct, thereby cutting down on the overall distance you need to travel.

Bushwhacking is the toughest way to go, and the easiest way to get lost. But it can pay off. Where I sometimes hunt elk, two parallel roaded canyons are separated by a steep divide for most of their length. Except for about three square miles in the middle, the divide bulges out into a rough circle of high hills. No roads or trails go into the area. A number of years ago I decided it was a good place to try tough hunting for easier elk.

From the east canyon road I set out up a steep draw that curved up behind a sea of hills. The hiking got more difficult as I climbed and the forest grew denser and more filled with downfall. About the time I was ready to call it quits, I stumbled onto a game trail that looked as if it had been bladed out by a machine. Fresh elk tracks by the dozens dappled its dirt. Here, less than a mile from a road used by numerous hunters, I'd bushwhacked into a spot where the elk felt secure, and I have since found them much easier to hunt there.

Hunting elk where they feel secure is not like hunting elk that are within sight and earshot of traffic and heavy hunting pressure. Elk like to keep on the move, and where they feel safe they do move—between half and three-quarters of a mile every couple of hours. Within a week's time they may remain within the same two square miles, but they're still always moving—even during daylight—when they aren't disturbed. This means that you're likely to find elk in a lot of different places, not just holed up in an impossible tangle of thick timber or a dog-hair patch of pole pine.

For food they're going to gravitate toward open south slopes or sparse forests where the most grass is available. They seem to prefer

Where hunting pressure is light, elk often bed down close to feeding areas in more open terrain.

the upper two-thirds of side slopes in moderate to large drainages. But in a drainage head where a steep, rocky headwall rises to meet the divide, the elk usually graze on the lower third of the slope.

Elk that are feeling secure with their surroundings often bed down close to where they feed, unlike heavily hunted elk, which sometimes move miles between nighttime feeding grounds and daytime cover.

Once, having hiked into elk country for several miles on a closed road, I set off down a forested ridge along which a natural opening on a broad terrace provided a likely feeding spot for elk. From above the opening I had a good view of the entire terrace. There wasn't an elk in sight. Still, I sat awhile, pulling out my binoculars to take a closer look.

The natural park was empty, all right, but as I continued to try to make elk sprout out of the grass where they obviously weren't going to grow, a movement at the edge of the meadow caught my attention. There, only a few feet back in the trees bordering the opening, was an elk. And then another and another. I counted close to a dozen elk—two with legal antlers—by the time I'd figured out where to look for them. They were taking a break from their feeding to chew their cuds. I waited and they eventually came back into the meadow to chow down again. The two miles I'd hiked in before starting to hunt definitely made for easier elk.

To hunt easier elk, first hike in whatever distance you figure elk will move to feel secure. Just hike, don't hunt unless you actually see an elk. Once you figure you've traveled that magical and somewhat illusory distance, leave the road behind. Logging roads are built to optimize the returns of logging operations, not to optimize the returns of elk hunting.

Once off the road, find a spot where you can spend up to an hour or more glassing surrounding terrain. As noted, you aren't going to find elk out in the middle of large clearcuts. Look for them along edges of forest cover. The larger the blocks of cover the more likely it is that elk will be using them.

Stand hunting can really pay off when you have a good vantage point over a lot of terrain in areas where elk are feeling at ease. They'll move more and use openings and sparse timber more. So just sitting and waiting for them to come to you may be your best tactic.

If sitting and glassing turns up nothing, it's time to start moving slowly through those likely places I've mentioned, places elk

Still-hunting slowly through likely feeding and bedding areas may be your only choice when glassing turns up nothing.

choose to forage and bed when they're feeling secure. But always keep an eye on how weather will influence their movement and activity.

Finally, where closed roads offer you access into easier elk hunting, give serious consideration to packing in your own "cart camp." It will allow you to be where the elk hunting is easier for a long stretch without the time-consuming bother of daily commutes.

I was first introduced to a cart camp by an elk specialist who'd designed a one-wheeled cart out of a bicycle wheel in order to pack camping gear along trails. I have since used a two-wheeled garden cart to pack a hunting camp in on a closed road. I got some strange looks from a few other hunters who were using the area. I also got an elk, which I packed out in two trips with the cart. The one other hunter who got an "easier elk" had to hire a horse packer to bring his out.

Carts, like this one designed for packing out game, are useful for bringing in heavy camping gear. (Cabela's)

192

BE PREPARED

When hunting without a guide in areas that are new to you, your chances of getting lost are real, even if you're hunting from a closed road. Be prepared with an emergency kit, carried at all times in a fannypack or backpack. The kit should include a compass, whistle, flares, matches, fire starter, space blanket, basic first-aid supplies, and high-energy food such as jerky and chocolate.

Most good elk hunting in the West is on public lands, particularly in national forests. Every national forest has a travel plan map showing road closures and the dates and reasons for the closures. Where closures are enforced during hunting season and where the reason for a closure is listed as "elk security," you'll find a good place to try tough hunting for easier elk.

Contact the Forest Service office in the area of the state you would like to hunt. In addition to travel plan maps, ask if they have similar interagency maps. These show road closures on all public lands, including national forests, BLM land, National Wildlife Refuges, and state lands.

WHERE TO GO

Bulls are present in both greater numbers and larger sizes in good habitat that's a mile or more from high hunting pressure, but there's still a lot of ground to cover, and knowing how elk use the land is critical. The following map will show you where you're most likely to find big bulls in Rocky Mountain elk habitat, from beginning to end of the rifle season.

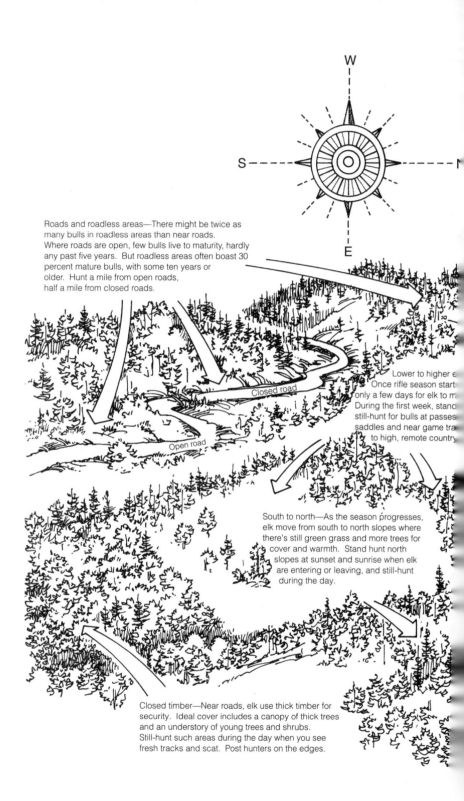

Roads and roadless areas—There might be twice as many bulls in roadless areas than near roads. Where roads are open, few bulls live to maturity, hardly any past five years. But roadless areas often boast 30 percent mature bulls, with some ten years or older. Hunt a mile from open roads, half a mile from closed roads.

Closed road

Open road

Lower to higher e
Once rifle season start
only a few days for elk to m
During the first week, stand
still-hunt for bulls at passes
saddles and near game tra
to high, remote country

South to north—As the season progresses, elk move from south to north slopes where there's still green grass and more trees for cover and warmth. Stand hunt north slopes at sunset and sunrise when elk are entering or leaving, and still-hunt during the day.

Closed timber—Near roads, elk use thick timber for security. Ideal cover includes a canopy of thick trees and an understory of young trees and shrubs. Still-hunt such areas during the day when you see fresh tracks and scat. Post hunters on the edges.

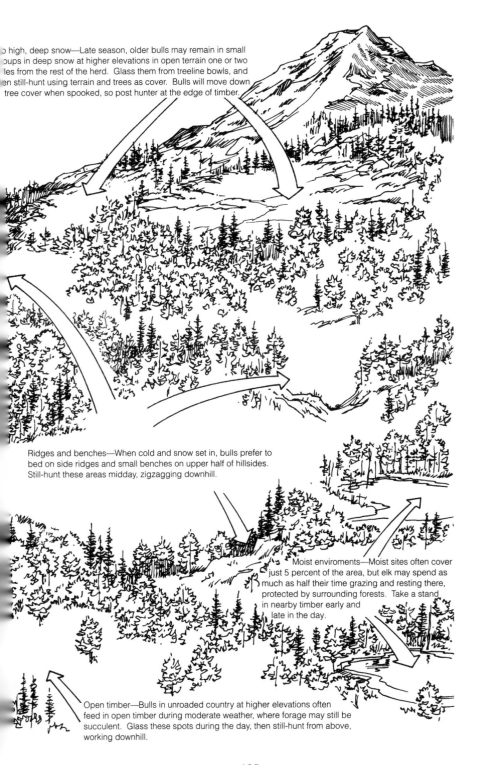

high, deep snow—Late season, older bulls may remain in small
oups in deep snow at higher elevations in open terrain one or two
les from the rest of the herd. Glass them from treeline bowls, and
en still-hunt using terrain and trees as cover. Bulls will move down
tree cover when spooked, so post hunter at the edge of timber.

Ridges and benches—When cold and snow set in, bulls prefer to
bed on side ridges and small benches on upper half of hillsides.
Still-hunt these areas midday, zigzagging downhill.

Moist enviroments—Moist sites often cover
just 5 percent of the area, but elk may spend as
much as half their time grazing and resting there,
protected by surrounding forests. Take a stand
in nearby timber early and
late in the day.

Open timber—Bulls in unroaded country at higher elevations often
feed in open timber during moderate weather, where forage may still be
succulent. Glass these spots during the day, then still-hunt from above,
working downhill.

195

FOOL ME ONCE

Bull elk that are bugled in by hunters, shot at, and missed often learn to avoid bugling hunters in the future.

Environmental Factors

Chapter 24

THE BENEFITS OF FIRE

It was a little before 3 PM when a district fire dispatcher notified Larry Keown that smoke was billowing from the forest south of Gardiner Lookout. As District Fire Management Officer with the U.S. Forest Service, Keown was responsible for overseeing all fires in the Noose Creek District of Idaho's Selway-Bitterroot Wilderness. The spreading flames crackled and spit on the steep southern slope of ponderosa pine above Bear Creek, a tributary of the Selway River. Keown knew the blaze had the potential of becoming an inferno, one that could engulf thousands of acres of trees and blot out the sun with its smoke.

He decided to let the fire burn. Its name became Independence.

The decision to let Independence run wild through the woods was the result of years of slowly changing attitudes toward the role of fire in land management. This and other "let burn" and "prescribed burn" decisions on public lands have been a long time in the making, but their positive effects on wildlife, especially big game, have been unquestionable. And the improved hunting opportunity fire has created is undeniable.

Around the turn of the last century, a series of nine catastrophic fires in the Great Lakes region took a devastating toll on human life and timber, killing a total of 3,400 people and consuming more than six million acres of forest land. This destruction helped incite a national mood that saw fire as an ugly force that had to be dealt with.

By 1934 the Forest Service had initiated its 10 AM Policy. This specified that all available firefighters and equipment be brought into action to suppress a forest fire by 10 AM the day after it started. In 1942 the Forest Service launched a massive nationwide fire-prevention drive. Three years later, Smokey the Bear was introduced to the public as the official spokesman for this effort. The now familiar "Only you can prevent forest fires" was his gruff warning.

The campaign has taught generation after generation that all fires—except well-controlled campfires—are bad news. According to the Forest Service, the number of wildfires and their destruction in total areas burned has dropped dramatically since the campaign first began. "Smokey has become one of the most effective campaigns in history . . . to influence a serious national problem," reports the organization.

Larry Keown kept a daily log of the Independence fire. And on July 10, six days after its beginning, Keown and Dave Clarke hiked into the wilderness to set up a base camp near the confluence of Cub and Bear Creeks, positioned within sight of the smoke and flames. To men for whom fire had always meant fire lines, machinery, and backbreaking work, it was a totally new experience.

"It was so quiet," Larry says, remembering. "There weren't any chain saws; no one was yelling. There was just the crackle of the fire, and once in a while a tree would crash to the ground."

For the last century the Forest Service has moved quickly to suppress forest fires. (USFWS)

For the next month, Clarke acted as a fire monitor, relaying fire and weather data via radio to the Noose Creek Ranger Station. Keown used this information to predict the erratic behavior of the growing blaze.

While Smokey the Bear was teaching us to bad-mouth forest fires, the use of fire suppression was teaching the Forest Service other things. Where fires were regularly extinguished, trees matured and died. As they began to fall and cover the ground, movement became difficult for elk and other large animals. While dead trees piled up on the forest floor, understory vegetation—in the absence of fire—grew to heights that were unreachable by browsing wildlife. Elk populations began to decline, and hunters were hard pressed to find game. With the accumulation of dead wood, the likelihood of wildfires began to escalate until they became inevitable in some areas. When they did occur, they raged in all-consuming fireballs that were extremely costly to combat.

As a result, the Forest Service began recognizing that fire could actually play a positive role in wildlife environs. For centuries, across the continent, Native Americans started fires to drive or surround deer while hunting. According to one report from the 1750s, tribes in the Southeast had an annual custom of fire hunting in October: " . . . hundreds of Indians . . . spreading themselves in length through a great extent of country, set the woods on fire, which with the assistance of the wind is driven to some peninsula, or neck of land, into which deers, bears and other animals were drove by the raging fire and smoak, and being hemm'd in are destroyed in great numbers by their guns."

Indians were also aware of fire's beneficial aftereffects. Tom Puchlerz of the Forest Service says, "Indians started a lot of fires; they understood that if they burned an area, they could come back later and it would be a good place to hunt."

Forest managers now understand that burned areas like this one can actually be very beneficial to elk and other wildlife, as well as to the long-term health of the forest.

Likewise, early settlers in the Southeast recognized that periodic fires promoted forage growth for wildlife, attracting game and giving hunters more success. When fires didn't occur naturally, homesteaders set them on purpose. In so doing, they became users of what has become known as prescribed burning—burning forests or plains under controlled conditions to achieve specific results.

In recent years, this technique has been developed by the Forest Service as an important tool to reduce wildfires and to improve wildlife habitats. For example, northern Idaho conifer forests offered little browse for elk until prescription burning was used in certain areas. Today shrubs grow where trees were burned, and elk use has increased dramatically. In some areas, winter elk use has risen over 300 percent. The increased game use, visibility, and ease of access caused by the burning have greatly improved hunting conditions.

Two weeks after starting, Independence had burned 682 acres. But before going out several months later, its effects were already becoming evident in new vegetation sprouting where the fire first began.

"Traveling upstream along Bear Creek was like walking through a time machine," recalls Keown. The vegetation that came back most rapidly were plants that had structural adaptations that could respond to fire. Plants with rhizomes, such as Oregon grape and kinnikinnick, for example, were quick to regenerate. Their horizontal, subsurface stems had been protected from the intense heat. Soon after the fire, they started sending up leafy shoots that were supplied with nutrients by roots that had remained unaffected by the flames.

The first new growth appeared where rocks had funneled water onto dormant rhizomes and root crowns. By October, protected with a mulch of scorched and fallen pine needles and fern fronds, wheatgrass would be four inches tall, and mountain maple saplings would reach three feet. Much of the rapid growth was due to the increase of nutrients present in the ash left by the burned vegetation.

It is this fire-equals-food equation that makes fire such a beneficial element in managing a variety of wildlife habitats. Increasingly, the Forest Service is setting fires and letting naturally caused fires burn in order to improve these habitats, and improved game habitats inevitably lead to improved hunting.

BRINGING IN THE ELK

Despite cinematic notions to the contrary, animals are rarely killed by fires. Although the aftereffects of fires occasionally produce conditions that favor some species over others, in most instances a heterogeneous and dynamic environment is created.

A fire doesn't normally devastate an entire area. Instead, it produces what is called a vegetative mosaic. As the fire travels over valleys and ridges, the terrain and the fuels in its path offer different conditions for burning, causing the fire to move in irregular patterns over the landscape. In some places, most of the vegetation may be destroyed; in others, just the ground cover or forest canopy may burn. The result is a mixture of vegetation of varying ages growing side by side. Elk gravitate to islands of unburned vegetation left inside a burn, and the irregular edges created by the fire allow them to feed comfortably in the open yet close to escape cover.

In addition to creating and maintaining a complete and healthy habitat, fire also creates various patterns of cover for hunters to use while stalking game.

Most important to the elk, however, is what a burn does to the food supply. Where fires have occurred, the new growth of both grasses and browse is highly digestible and nutritious—up to 50 percent more nutritious than before the fire. This boost continues for an average of three years after the burn.

Fire scars found on Douglas firs at elevations between 5,000 and 8,600 feet in Wyoming indicate that wildfires may have burned every twenty to twenty-five years before we started extinguishing them. On the plains, natural fires may have occurred as frequently as every ten years, suggesting that grassland can also be improved by periodic burning.

Elk quickly pick up on a good place to eat, and there are many instances of high increases in elk concentrations caused by the effects of burns. Keown shared one particularly dramatic example with me. A few years ago, he was involved with a prescribed burn of hundreds of acres in central Montana. It was an area that had previously been used by elk only during severe winter storms.

But after the burn elk moved into the area and actually established a resident herd. Larry attributes this to the higher quality forage and browse produced by the fire.

Or consider the Sun River Game Range near Choteau, Montana, where approximately three thousand elk winter on a mixture of native plants. Rough fescue, a perennial bunchgrass, is their favorite. But in some areas of the range, the accumulation of old-growth grassland and dead plant litter impeded elk access to new growth, and what they could find was poor in nutrition. As a result, six hundred acres of the old-growth grassland were set ablaze, creating a subsequent 300 percent increase in elk use.

A similar prescription burn was set in the Elkhorn Mountains near Helena, Montana, in an attempt to regenerate old-growth grassland, which elk had not been using. Of particular

Highly nutritious grasses and other vegetation will soon grow here, attracting elk from far and wide.

interest is the fact that half of the cost of this Elkhorn burn was paid for by the Helena Chapter of the Rocky Mountain Elk Foundation, a private organization dedicated to the preservation of elk, elk habitat, and elk hunting. Through a new Forest Service Challenge Grant created by Congress, the Rocky Mountain Elk Foundation (http://rmef.org) has provided hundreds of thousands of dollars for habitat improvement and has become the Forest Service's biggest grant matcher.

Despite the success stories over the rediscovery of the beneficial effects of fire for wildlife habitats and for improved elk-hunting opportunities, some shortsighted uses of prescribed burns have occurred.

One Forest Service official in Montana admits: "There's a lot of controversy as far as burning sagebrush because the mule deer are tied pretty heavily to it. In a lot of cases it's providing some pretty good cover. We made some mistakes in the late 1970s; we burned up some sagebrush that should never have been burned. It was really tall stuff that was providing really good cover for mule deer, but we were trying to improve grass production for elk and forgot about the deer.

"We've laid off sagebrush lately," says the official. "Fire can produce a lot of grass. You can get a lot of elk coming in there right away. But you have to think about the trade-offs on other species."

The use of fire for wildlife is here to stay, despite the admonitions of Smokey the Bear. But the problem now, according to one Forest Service researcher, is "reeducating the public on the ecological soundness of the role fire has played in the maintenance of natural ecosystems in much of the U.S." That problem of reeducation has been exacerbated recently by extreme fire seasons in 1999, when 5,661,976 acres burned; 2000, when 8,422,237 acres burned; and 2002, when 6,937,584 acres burned nationally. The prescribed burn that got out of control in New Mexico in

2000, burning 47,650 acres and 235 structures, did not help matters either.

Despite the severity of recent fire seasons and the questions they raise in the minds of a jittery public, the fires in many cases have changed the distribution of elk on their habitat. "Forage is often improved for several years after fires on grasslands," says Kurt Alt, wildlife biologist for Montana Fish, Wildlife & Parks. "And where forest succession is set back to the shrub stage that positive effect may last longer." So it's worth researching where recent fires have burned within existing elk habitat when planning your next hunt. Elk concentrations are likely to be higher in those areas.

As for the Independence fire, eight months after its birth by lightning the last of it was seen burning in a lone pine, spotted by an employee of the Idaho Department of Fish and Game conducting an elk survey. There is no doubt that the effects of fires like Independence remain a boon to elk and the people who hunt them for years afterwards.

Chapter 25

A CLEARCUT MYTH

The day before the opening of big-game season several years ago, I packed a light camp into a 7,500-foot divide between two major drainages in southwestern Montana. My campsite was selected as much for aesthetic reasons as it was for hunting tactics, for I could see the snow-dusted peaks of high mountains as well as the tawny grasses of a nearby natural meadow. It was the type of small ridgeside park that elk favor on clear, frost-cleansed mornings in early fall. Grasses along the clearing edge were still green, yet thick east-slope timber below offered ideal escape cover.

Although there were a number of other such meadows along the divide, this one came with an important extra feature. At the south end of the open park, the ridgeline dipped down into the timber to form a gentle saddle between the two drainages. And I had reason to believe elk would be using it come morning.

My thinking was simple. The drainage to the east had a road up the bottom from which other roads branched to traverse large sections of cut-over land. I could see some of the irregular checkerboard pattern of the forest and clearcuts from where I sat. The roads provided easy access into prime elk country, and the clearcuts had good forage in areas where a hunter could see well and get a clear shot. It was an area that attracted many of the local hunters.

The drainage to the west was unroaded and thick with timber interspersed with small open meadows. It took hours of hard hiking to reach, and if you did get an elk in this drainage, it might take days to get it out.

Before dawn on opening morning, a procession of headlights flickered up from the east drainage like a torchlight parade as vehicles branched out onto logging roads on either side of the canyon. And at daybreak a fusillade of shots echoed up to my ears and then subsided to occasional pops. By 9:30 the first elk were filtering up through the firs below the meadow. A few stopped to crop green grass at the forest edge before slipping over the saddle into the cover and quiet of the adjacent canyon. The procession had just begun.

There was no doubt that all the hunters in the timber cuts below would find easier hunting than I, but not one would find as many elk.

Clearcuts and elk—it has long been thought that they go together like bread and butter. Cutting blocks of timber in stretches of woodland from Maine to Oregon opens up the forest canopy so new grasses and forage plants can grow, providing a plentiful and attractive new source of food for elk. In addition, logging roads provide access for hunters into otherwise remote game habitat where they can hunt the timber edges formed by clearcuts, which attract elk.

Twenty years ago, I believed this theory. Fifteen years ago, I was finding some flaws in it. Today my experiences and the results of some long-term studies have put a lot of qualifications on what turned out to be rather sloppy generalizations.

Serious scientific doubts started being cast on the supposed clearcut-game partnership in the early 1960s when, as one

Although many hunters still believe that clearcuts are good areas to find elk, the reality is that elk usually avoid such areas, particularly where nearby logging roads are still open to vehicles. (USFWS)

researcher put it, "Wildlife managers [were] often confounded by the absence of elk in areas with obvious forage surpluses," specifically clearcuts. It was this sort of concern that initiated the Montana Cooperative Elk-Logging Study years ago. Conducted by the Montana Department of Fish, Wildlife & Parks, the Forestry School of the University of Montana, the BLM, the Forest Service, and the Plum Creek Timber Company, this fifteen-year study probably represents the most extensive research on the relationship between timber cutting and elk habitat use done anywhere.

At any rate, while the wildlife management community was busy looking into the relationship between clearcuts and elk, I—quite ignorant of their efforts—was beginning to raise some questions of my own, as a hunter. My first suspicions that something might be awry in this relationship began years ago when I decided to hunt elk in a new timber cut at the head of a local drainage. Although logging was still being done in the area, the weekend seemed to provide a quiet time to take advantage of this new access into prime elk habitat. And for two days I glassed and walked and took stands near cut-over edges where new forage was clearly visible and very plentiful.

Not only did I not see any elk, I did not see any signs of elk, nor did the other hunters I talked with that weekend. I attributed this obvious absence of wildlife to the fact that logging was still being done in the area. And the Montana Elk-Logging Study gave credence to that speculation by concluding that logging operations do displace elk.

As a matter of fact, some big operations, where logging roads are open to non-logging traffic, may move elk up to four miles away and into other drainages. With smaller operations, displacement may be closer to half a mile. But in all cases elk move far enough away to lose visual contact with men and equipment. And in most cases, the elk don't return until men and equipment have left the area.

I've also found that elk aren't likely to use clearcuts as long as logging roads are left open to any public traffic. I recall one morning when I planned to hunt along the edge of a timbered area adjoining an old stand of fir. The timber provided excellent cover and escape avenues, while the cut was rich in forage. It seemed an ideal location for elk.

After carefully parking my truck in the trees near the lower edge of the clearing, I started still-hunting the periphery of the timber with plans to work around the entire cut until I came back to the truck. And I did make the complete circuit, but by the time I'd completed it, I was convinced I was hunting in the wrong spot. Although I'd seen only one vehicle drive up the road that traversed the cut, at least half a dozen noisy pickups had moaned up the grade out of sight but within easy earshot.

By this time, clearcuts were starting to lose their initial appeal.

By way of confirmation, one mule deer researcher told me that "anytime hunting season's going on, in most cases, there's not going to be a lot of deer activity on the edge of a significant clearcut because of its association with roads." Elk may be even more adversely influenced. "In central Montana," according to the elk-logging study, "roads passing through clearcuts depressed elk use of the opening by up to 90 percent."

Nevertheless, it is sometimes very difficult to give up on something that for so many reasons seems like such a good thing. So, up to ten years ago, I continued to try my luck at hunting clearcuts. There was even a time when I was convinced I'd gotten into some elk.

It happened in the middle of the morning during the first week of the season. I'd been following the edges of a large cut down off a ridge and had come to the bottom where a creek ran back through the timber about seventy-five yards away. In some mud at the side of the clearing were several sets of tracks, partially filled with water, that I was sure had been made by elk.

The sight of the tracks had an immediate heightening effect on my heart rate, and I set off in the direction they led without taking notice of some other signs that would have quickly de-flated my pulse. It wasn't until I'd covered a good fifty yards that the brown pie-sized puddings at my feet registered Herefords in my brain, and I stumbled to a stop, feeling as foolish as a kid who'd just fumbled his first kiss.

As it turned out, there was more of import to the cattle tracks than I suspected at the time. The Montana Elk-Logging Study puts it succinctly if somewhat academically: "Systematic observation revealed a significant tendency for elk to avoid cattle." In fact, the chances of elk using a clearcut along with cattle are about half what they would be in the absence of cattle. And even if cattle are removed from the area before hunting season opens, they've eaten and trampled so much forage that the site is of little use to elk. One study estimated that "cattle grazing during summer removed 64 to 88 percent of available herbage on sites by fall."

And there were some other problems I ran into in my experiences with hunting timbered areas. There were times late in the hunting season when I tried to move around the open edges of timbered areas and simply got bogged down in deep snow. Moving under the cover of nearby trees, I found snow accumulations shallower and the walking easier. Elk seem to find the same thing, and they stay under the protection of the forest.

Where thick timber slash has been left on the ground after a logging operation, I've found similar problems with movement. It seems that elk do as well. The study revealed that clearcuts between two and ten years old in areas of minimum human disturbance that are near extensive timber stands and that have been cleared of logging slash by burning were found to be best suited for elk. However, if these cuts aren't already in or near traditional fall range, elk aren't likely to bother using them.

And so, after years of trying, I've given up on clearcuts. It has become clear to me that elk don't particularly like them or the disturbances they bring where logging roads remain open to traffic.

I have not, however, given up on using logging roads. That camp I made the day before elk season I packed in from the end of a logging road not more than a mile away. It took me about half an hour to get to the campsite from my vehicle. Had I come in the old way it would have taken me two or three hours.

Areas like this, where cattle have grazed during the summer months, tend to be less productive for elk.

The fact is that while elk are rarely found along logging roads or clearcuts themselves, access to elk habitat has been opened up by the vast road system logging has created. Where once a hunter had to horsepack or hike miles to find the heart of a game range, now he can drive on logging rods to within a mile or two of where elk can be found.

For example, last fall, after the first good snow, I drove up a local logging road that parallels one of the many creek bottoms in the area. At the point where a prominent side ridge cut a right angle from the road and led up toward the divide, I parked my vehicle and started climbing the ridge. Actually, for the first quarter of a mile it was more like shinnying up the ridge—it was that steep and that littered with downed timber beneath the thick northeast forest canopy.

But gradually the ridge tamed down, and I found myself walking the grade with little difficulty. The sights and sounds of the road were obliterated by the nose of the ridge, and the country seemed as remote as it would be 10 miles from road's end. Yet I was no more than a mile from my car.

Near the top of the ridge I cut fresh elk tracks and, a few minutes later, fresh blood. Someone had gotten there before me. His tracks joined the elk tracks another fifty yards up the ridge. On top of the divide, I found the hunter with a fine five-point bull. Like me, the fellow had hiked up a side ridge away from the clearcuts and the roads and had dropped over the divide into the adjacent unroaded canyon. The elk had been bedded on a terrace toward the top of the divide and had headed for the thicker east-slope timber when it was shot.

This was an area where I've never failed to see elk or their fresh tracks, despite the proximity to clearcuts and logging roads. But it's an area that combines several important ingredients. First, and perhaps most important, it is protected from the sights and sounds of traffic and logging operations by thick timber and steep topography. Those disturbances are nearby, but the elk are not aware of them.

Second, the two sides of the divide have ideal aspects. The unroaded side faces southeast and has natural open parklands and sparse timber where forage for elk is ideal and where the sun's warmth melts snow and provides heat even on cold clear days. The roadbed, clearcut side of the divide faces northeast and is very thick with timber right to the top of the divide, where logging has not been done.

With forage, radiant heat, and easy movement on one side of the divide and thick escape cover plus protection from radiant heat loss on the other side, elk can find satisfaction for their needs provided, again, that they can't see or hear the disturbances associated with clearcuts and logging roads. There are similar situations to be found close to almost any areas that have been opened up by logging roads. And these are the places to hunt elk—not the clearcuts themselves.

Since most logging roads in the West are on public land, you can use district national forest maps to locate uncut areas to which the roads provide access. Then you can look on the maps for features of topography, aspect, and vegetation that will provide elk with good forage, security, and comfort.

Logging roads that end close to the top of a ridge but don't drop into an adjacent unroaded drainage are the real bonanzas to look for. They allow the closest approach to prime hunting country. And they let you start hunting down ridges almost immediately, a tactic that gives you a definite edge on the game.

Still, there's no free lunch. The clearcut-game partnership has been proven largely mythical. You have to get off the clearcuts and logging roads and hump the hills. But using a logging road for part of the way will allow you a lot more hunting time while eating up a lot less time just getting there.

Chapter 26

HOW OTHER ANIMALS AFFECT ELK

COMPETITION

Elk, whitetails, and mule deer are the three most sought after big-game animals in the U.S. Although hunters compete for these species every season, we don't tend to think of the animals competing among themselves. But, on occasion, they do.

Their range and the range of other wild and domestic ungulates overlap in many areas of the country. Elk may share their living space with as many as seven other wild ungulates, including whitetails, mule deer, moose, bighorn sheep, mountain goats, and even pronghorns. When two or more of these species compete for the same food supply, one of them may face malnutrition or starvation.

Fortunately, over centuries of interactions wild animals have developed patterns of habitat use in which species sharing the same range have their own separate niches. Differences in habits, cover use, and food preference usually prevent them from directly competing with one another for the same space or forage.

Where elk share the same landscape with whitetails and mu-leys, whitetails usually prefer to feed along brushy stream bot-toms; mule deer browse under the forest cover; and elk go for the grasses on open hills.

When competition does occur among deer and elk, how-ever, the elk seem to be the best survivors. Their ability to eat and easily digest a wider variety of foods than whitetails and mule deer gives them a definite competitive edge. Elk can also handle greater snow depths than deer and by nature are more mobile, covering more ground and gaining access to more food. Deer, on the other hand, have much smaller home ranges, which they may refuse to leave even in the face of dwindling food supplies.

While native wild animals have had millennia to adapt to one another's patterns of land use, the introduction of domestic

Mule deer often inhabit the same territory as elk, but rarely do local populations threaten elk survival. However, cattle grazing has a much more noticeable effect. (USFWS)

livestock to the equation is a relatively new variable. It wasn't until the 1860s and 1870s that cattle and sheep were run widely on western rangelands. Their numbers and distribution have not been determined by natural forces, but by ranchers and government agencies.

In some cases, the results have been detrimental to elk. Much elk range in the West is grazed by livestock for at least part of the year. As recently as 1975, a third of the public western rangeland was rated in poor or bad condition. Only 17 percent was rated good or excellent. Elk suffer under such conditions, because both elk and cattle prefer to feed on grass.

Recent use of rest/rotation grazing systems by ranches in the West has greatly improved forage for livestock and elk, however. Under these systems three or four grazing units are used or rested throughout the year. Some years a unit may have no grazing at all. The increase in elk use on these ranches has caused headaches for ranchers, sometimes resulting in special "depredation" hunts that elk hunters should look into when reviewing hunting regulations.

Also of interest to hunters is the indication from some studies that elk have a social intolerance for cattle. The study referenced in the last chapter on clearcuts concluded that, in any habitat, elk are only half as likely to use an area where there are cattle as they are to use an area where cattle are absent.

Even after livestock have been removed from public grazing allotments in the early fall, elk seem reluctant to make use of areas during the hunting season that have been grazed and trampled by cattle. Hunters should take this into consideration when they are deciding which hunting areas are best suited for finding elk.

However, the bottom line in the elk/cattle equation is the reality that human tolerance is the ultimate limiting factor in the size of elk populations in the West. With the majority of winter elk range existing in private ranchland in many states, ranchers end up having elk on their property for a good part of the winter. It is their tolerance for elk, and their cooperation with fish and game departments, that allows hunters continued elk-hunting possibilities in many areas.

PREDATION

Historically, hunters have seesawed in their attitude toward predators and predation. During the first half of the last century, the general feeling was that whatever game the wolves, coyotes, mountain lions, and bears killed meant that much less game for the hunter. Bounties and predator-control programs all but wiped out the wolves, and they put a good dent in the mountain lion population. More recently, however, popular opinion has it that predators help keep game population in balance with the carrying capacity of their ranges and that predators have been getting a bad rap.

The truth seems to lie somewhere in between.

The greatest effect natural predators, including coyotes, mountain lions, and bears—and now wolves once again—have on elk populations occurs in the spring. This is because newborn calves are more vulnerable to predation than any other age group. For example, of fifty-three elk calves radio-collared within a week of birth in Idaho, twenty-eight were killed by black bears within a few weeks.

With the reintroduction of wolves in Montana, Wyoming, and Idaho, many hunters feared a drastic decline in the elk population from wolf predation. And, in fact, over the last ten years biologists have seen elk numbers in Yellowstone National

Park drop from 19,045 to 8,335, with a calf survival rate of only about 50 percent. Many sportsmen pointed accusing fingers at the wolves. But in the first two years of a three-year study titled "Multi-Trophic Level Ecology of Wolves, Elk, and Vegetation in Yellowstone National Park," wolves haven't been the real bad guy.

In 2003, the first year of the study, fifty-one newborn elk were tagged and only seventeen survived. Nineteen were confirmed killed by black or grizzly bears, five by wolves, three by coyotes, three by natural or other causes, two more by either bears or wolves, one by a mountain lion, and one by a wolverine. In 2004, forty-four calves were tagged and just thirteen survived. Eighteen were killed by black or grizzly bears, four by

Many hunters feared that the reintroduction of wolves would decimate elk populations throughout the West, but so far studies have shown that bears are the primary culprit in the loss of elk calves. (USFWS)

coyotes, three by wolves, two by unknown predators, two by natural or other causes, one by either a bear or a wolf, and one by a golden eagle.

The preliminary results seem to indicate that hunters should worry more about bears when it comes to elk predation, at least on newborn calves in the spring.

Winter, on the other hand, favors the predator's ability to prey on older elk. Where snow has crusted enough to support predators such as coyotes, wolves, and dogs but is not strong enough to hold the weight of an elk, even healthy adult animals can be taken down. The above study found that bears hunt in a systematic pattern, looking for hiding calves in the spring and fall. Wolves usually attack calves when they're with larger groups of elk in the fall and winter.

Although free-roaming dogs, including "faithful" family pets, may cause little direct predation on elk, their harassment of game can have more subtle effects. Elk may be forced to concentrate on more secure niches of their home range, increasing competition for food and forcing them onto more marginal habitat. In northern climates, according to one wildlife manager, harassment by domestic dogs "can also result in [elk] moving longer distances to feed at night when temperatures are lower and energy losses are higher."

So while the dog harassment may not result specifically in mortality, it can cause enough stress to make elk susceptible to death from disease and starvation.

What all this means to the hunter is that predators can significantly reduce local game populations in some areas of the country during certain years. Start by recognizing that the effects of predation are largely dependent on such variables as age and health of the prey, predator/prey ratios, and weather conditions.

Harassment by predators can indirectly affect elk stocks by leaving animals more vulnerable to starvation and disease.

And factor in this information when planning your next fall outing for elk.

Where serious depredations occur, the question for hunters and game managers is whether predator control can increase the number of elk available to hunters and whether killing predators is an acceptable way to bring about this increase.

PURGE LEAFY SPURGE

In some areas of the West, weeds are threatening to crowd out the native grasses that grow on winter elk range. The nastiest culprit is leafy spurge, which has the potential to reduce forage production on bunchgrass range by as much as 90 percent. Leafy spurge's twenty-foot taproot resists chemical control, and attempts to cut or dig it out may result in greater infestations, since even a small piece of chopped-up root can sprout into a new plant.

An exotic plant brought into the U.S. years ago by seeds stuck on the clothing and belongings of European immigrants, leafy spurge has been spread throughout the West by vehicles, people, and animals, all of which unknowingly carry the seeds.

In an attempt to get a handle on the problem, the Forest Service is insisting that outfitters carry certified weed-free hay for saddle horses and pack animals entering national forests.

Although elk (and deer and cattle) turn up their noses at leafy spurge, sheep and goats like to eat it. So these animals are being used to keep the weed under control in parts of Idaho and Montana. In addition, the Rocky Mountain Elk Foundation is working with the Forest Service to chemically eradicate leafy spurge on elk winter range in Madison Gulch, Montana.

Sportsmen can help prevent the spread of spurge by using certified weed/seed-free forage and straw and by reporting any sightings of this weed, characterized by its yellowish-green flowers—even small infestations—to the Forest Service. *Continued on next page*

Research is presently being done on the use of a fungus that may stop the weed from spreading. Another hope for the future is a borer beetle that destroys the plant by eating its way down through the taproot. So in the future, don't be surprised if you hear the cry, "Bring on the beetles!"

Chapter 27

WHERE HAVE ALL THE
BIG ONES GONE?

"Where have all the big ones gone?" It's a question that may be as old as hunting. You hear it from old-timers at two-pump rural gas stations and from youngsters just cutting their hunting teeth. More often than not the state fish and game departments take the rap for the lack, or the apparent lack, of big bulls.

Responding to pointed fingers, the Department of Fish, Wildlife & Parks here in Montana recently investigated the matter of big bulls, and its findings—valid for most states—should be considered by any hunter.

Although hunting regulations certainly can influence the quantity and quality of big bulls, there are a number of natural regulating factors that game managers have no influence over. Weather is a major consideration. First, in general, bulls naturally do not live as long as cows. Like actuarial tables for our own species, the males in the population show a shorter average life span than females. Male elk die earlier for the same reason human males do—stress.

Bulls are subjected to the most stress at the worst time of year. They laze about doing nothing all summer long, but when fall comes around they shift into full gear for the rut. They're constantly on the run, they get into fights, and they don't eat nourishing food, if they eat at all. The older the bull and the more clout he has in the herd, the harder he drives himself. Consequently, a bull goes into winter physically run down. He's tired and has lost a lot of fat reserves. Many bulls, especially the older ones, simply don't make it through periods of harsh weather in this condition.

While many mature males don't survive because of the weather, many young bulls don't survive to maturity for the same reason. The number of big males in a population at any given time is largely dependent on how many male calves survived four to six years earlier. Harsh weather conditions, like droughts or blizzards or exceedingly cold temperatures over long periods or just long snowy winters, can wipe out a large percentage of a yearly calf crop.

So harsh weather—often forgotten or only dimly remembered by hunters—can result in a lack of males many years down the line.

Weather also affects plant growth, which plays a role in nutrition, which influences antler growth. When forage growth is retarded in any elk habitat because of lack of water or because of untimely frosts or other weather-related conditions, antler growth may also be stunted because available food lacks suitable nutrition.

Weather also can be responsible for a *perceived* absence of bulls. Harsh conditions tend to concentrate elk and make them more visible to hunters, while unusually mild weather during the hunting season may keep game dispersed, allowing animals to remain on parts of their range not normally frequented by hunters.

Undersized antlers are more the result of poor forage in a given year than the age of the bull.

For example, one fall in southwestern Montana, the weather remained warm and dry throughout most of the season. In places where I can normally count on getting at least a glimpse of some bulls, I saw none, nor did most hunters in the area. It was a situation that prompted some to wonder out loud: "Where have all the bulls gone?"

A scant six weeks from the end of that hunting season, I could drive out by the open foothills near where I hunted earlier and see elk coming out of the timber—sixty, maybe seventy head—and among them were some fine bulls. They'd been somewhere nearby all the time.

Other influences, non-hunting human influences, can lead to low male:female ratios and to fewer big males. Some of these include urban sprawl and its accompanying roads and highway systems, timber harvesting, mining, and gas and oil exploration and development, along with the increased traffic that goes with all these human activities. These sorts of developments often occur in areas close to elk winter ranges. And it puts additional stress on the animals at a time when the males in particular are already in poor shape.

There is no doubt that hunting also has played a role in reducing the percentage of big bulls available to hunters. Across the country, the number of elk hunters has increased in the past thirty years. But this increase hasn't been followed by an increase in big bulls, since elk populations in most areas during the past decade have been at or near the carrying capacities of their habitats. As a result, an increasing number of hunters have been looking for a relatively fixed number of bulls. This means that out of the total hunting population a lower percentage of hunters will have a chance of coming home with a big bull than they did in "the good old days."

In addition, with the increase in hunters over the past decades there has been an increase in roads, especially logging

If hunters want to see a higher proportion of big racks, like the ones on these Tule elk, they may have to submit to increased limitations on hunting opportunity. (USFWS)

roads in the West, which have facilitated access. This increased access has meant a decrease in security for elk. And where hunting regulations have not become more restrictive, mature bulls have decreased in number because of increased hunting pressure.

So in many areas of many states there are fewer big bulls because up until recently most states have managed for general hunting opportunities and for game population control, not for big bulls.

Consequently, when someone asks, "Where have all the big ones gone?" we have to answer, "Those that nature or human development haven't taken, we the hunters have."

The natural question to follow, of course, is whether or not something should be done about the shrinking male population and at what cost.

Although low male:female ratios may be acceptable from a biological point of view, some hunters want to see more and bigger bulls. But the only way to attain this objective seems to be to limit the number of hunters. Mandatory waiting periods after harvesting a bull, closed elk season during rut, quota systems on big bulls, limited vehicle access, increased antlerless hunting, and limited permits are all possibilities. There are others. Each one has a long list of positive and negative implications. The one common denominator, however, is that all of these management strategies result in limiting hunter opportunity in one way or another, a situation that is not necessarily bad but one that should be recognized. A permit system, for example, would give game managers the greatest control over attaining their objectives. On the other hand, it would put the most limitations on hunter opportunity. In addition, most of the management strategies designed to increase the number and size of bulls are costly to implement and administer.

Perhaps most important to realize is that a great deal of research data is needed in order to tailor an effective management strategy to fit the idiosyncrasies of a particular hunting area. That takes time, effort, and money to collect. Also, before implementing a management strategy it is necessary to know how many bulls there are to begin with and in what age group. And then you must monitor that population information from year to year to see if the management strategy is working.

As one wildlife biologist put it: "If you are going to have a successful trophy bull management area, the price tag for each one of those bulls killed is going to be significantly higher than for your general maximum-opportunity, either-sex season."

So the bottom line is this: We're going to have to accept these costs and the inherent limitations on our hunting opportunities if we want to see more and bigger bulls.

Planning Your Hunt

Chapter 28

SELECTING A RIFLE OR BOW

Choosing an elk rifle can be as complicated as you want to make it. You can consult multitudes of experts and study reports, charts, and ballistics tables. You can read the stars and the cards and quiz friends, acquaintances, and complete strangers. You can agonize over half a dozen or more rifles. But selecting a rifle doesn't really have to be difficult. I prefer to keep the whole process simple.

Start by considering the game you're after. An elk is bigger than a whitetail or mule deer. Muleys run between 150 and 350 pounds. If you get into an exceptional buck, he may push 400 pounds. But a big bull elk may weigh in at 800 pounds or more—in the neighborhood of a half-ton pickup.

Also, consider the distances at which you're likely to be shooting. You may get shots at forest-dwelling elk that will be measured in dozens of yards. In open parkland or sparse timber, however, you might be shooting at elk hundreds of yards away. Still, the thrill of elk hunting, as I hope I've imparted in these pages, is in cultivating the ability and the know-how to get close to them. With that in mind, any shot over 200 yards is a long shot—too long a shot in my book.

So what kind of rifle will you need to effectively down an 800-pound elk at 200 yards with one shot? I add the qualifier of a single shot because you'll want the elk on the ground after one shot. It may run fifty to a hundred yards on sheer adrenaline after it is shot, but it will most likely be running too fast to take pot shots at before it collapses. So think one shot, which also forces you to think about getting as close as you can to your game before you pull the trigger. That's a lot of what elk hunting should be about.

A bolt-action rifle is perfect for that one shot. You aren't going to need the speed that other actions may offer for popping cartridges in and out. A bolt action is also more dependable and safer than other actions.

To further simplify the choice in a rifle, I like to direct elk hunters to some no-nonsense advice from the Alaska Department of Fish and Game website (http://www.state.ak.us/adfg): "If you presently own a rifle chambered for the .270 Winchester, 7mm–08, .308 Winchester or .30–06 and can place all your shots in an eight-inch circle out to 200 yards from a sitting or kneeling position you can be a successful Alaskan hunter. To be as effective as possible these cartridges should be loaded with premium quality bullets such as the Nosler Partition. If hit in the heart-lung area with a 180-grain Nosler Partition fired from a .30–06, the bullet will pass completely through a mature bull moose, interior grizzly, or black bear."

And, of course, it will pass completely through a trophy bull elk whether the bull lives in Alaska or the Lower Forty-Eight.

Bolt actions like this Remington Model 710 are dependable and accurate.

The website goes on to say that the keys to being a successful big-game hunter are physical conditioning and shooting accuracy. So magnum rifles are simply not needed (and may be counterproductive because of recoil and noise) for even the heavyweight game of Alaska.

"The two most common complaints of professional Alaskan guides are hunters who are not in good physical condition and hunters who cannot accurately shoot their rifles. Because they do not practice enough they cannot shoot accurately enough. They miss their best chance at taking their dream animal or, worse yet, they wound and lose an animal. Most experienced guides prefer the hunter to come to camp with a .270 or .30–06 rifle they can shoot well rather than a shiny new magnum that has been fired just enough to get sighted-in."

Let me just add that all the elk I have shot in over thirty years of hunting have been cleanly downed with a .30–06 firing a 180-grain bullet. So just keep it simple.

Finally, a good elk rifle should have a quality scope. Variable-power scopes have become the standard these days. A modern 3X–9X scope offers a bright, full-field view of that elk without a lot of head bobbing necessary to find the exact position for clarity. You don't need any higher magnification than 9X (something like 2.5X–8X or 3X–10X are also fine), because as you go higher your in-focus range gets pushed out farther. For example, with an adjustable objective lens focused at 200 yards on a 14X scope, objects closer than 150 yards are going to be blurry.

A decent rifle/scope combination these days could end up costing around a thousand dollars ($600–$700 for the rifle, $300–$400 for the scope). A really fancy rifle/scope combo could run three thousand dollars. But it's your money. You may already have a perfectly fine elk rifle, one you've used for years, in which case you won't need to spend a dime.

Modern compounds send arrows at speeds of around 300 feet per second, but bowhunters still need to shoot accurately from within 25 to 30 yards to ensure a quick, clean kill. (Cabela's)

There are, of course, alternatives to the modern rifle for hunting elk. If you are fanatic about elk hunting, and are skilled with a bow, you can start archery hunting at the beginning of September here in Montana, for example.

As an archer, you'll have to bring into play your best bugling skills and your knowledge of elk habits and habitats to get close enough—twenty to thirty yards—for an accurate shot with a bow with a 60- to 65-pound draw weight. Don't feel you need a "magnum" bow, something in the 70- to 80-pound range. As in the case of rifles, use a bow you can handle easily, comfortably, and accurately, whether it's a traditional longbow or recurve or a fancy new compound bow with the latest cams. And whether you use a bow or a rifle, keep this motto in mind: a clean kill with a single shot. You owe it to yourself and the elk you hunt.

ELK HUNTERS ATTRACT GRIZZLY BEARS

Elk hunters in Montana and Wyoming may be changing the fall distribution of some grizzlies that live near Yellowstone National Park, according to a report by the Interagency Grizzly Bear Study Team. The team investigated movements of radio-marked bears in the vicinity of the Park's southern and northern boundaries before and during the 1983 to 2000 hunting seasons. They found that when hunting season opened, marked bears were more than twice as likely to be outside the Park, and they attribute this to the availability of gut piles left by hunters. Annually, hunters in the area surrounding Yellowstone leave on the ground an estimated 370 tons of elk remains, which grizzlies avidly feed upon.

Continued on next page

Conflicts with bears have been on the rise recently. Take the proper precautions when hunting where grizzly populations are high, particularly after your elk is on the ground. (USFWS)

The fall congregation of bears and hunters has increased confrontations, resulting in some hunter maulings and some bear deaths. During the last decade, hunting incidents were the single largest source of known human-caused bear mortalities. Hunters should take additional precautions in the way they hunt and handle carcasses in grizzly country. Here are recommendations for hunters in grizzly country (provided by Montana Fish, Wildlife & Parks).

CARRY BEAR PEPPER SPRAY AND KNOW HOW TO USE IT

- Hunting puts you at risk of encountering grizzlies. Elk bugling, game calls, and cover scents may attract bears.

- If you hunt alone in grizzly country let someone know your detailed plans and periodically check in. Hunting partners should share details of their hunt plans and have a check-in or communication system. If you feel uneasy hunting alone in grizzly country, hunt side-by-side with a partner.

- Pay attention to fresh bear sign. Communicate with other hunters and let them know when grizzly bears have been seen and/or fresh sign observed.

- Some grizzly bears may move in the direction of gunshots because they have learned to associate the sound with a gut pile or animal carcass.

Continued on next page

- The golden rule is "get the elk or deer out of the area as quickly as possible." The longer a carcass remains lying on the ground, hung up in hunting camp, or in the back of a truck, the more likely it will be discovered by a grizzly. The sooner the animal is taken home, the better.

- Carcasses left for a period of time require special precautions. Carry a colored, lightweight tarp or space blanket. Put the guts on the tarp and drag them at least a few hundred feet away from the carcass. Then use the tarp to cover the carcass to discourage birds and a bear's attention to the carcass. Locate an observation point two hundred yards (if possible) away from the carcass with a clear line of sight. Before leaving, walk to the observation point and memorize the site.

- When returning, approach the observation point carefully. Yell or whistle repeatedly. With binoculars, study the scene from the observation point and scan the area for the carcass and any movement. If a grizzly bear is at the site and refuses to leave or the meat has been covered with debris by a bear and is not salvageable, report the incident to [the nearest fish and game office]. Hunters who have lost an animal to a grizzly may be eligible for another license.

- Do not attempt to frighten away or haze a grizzly.

- Bears are opportunists and change their behavior in order to take advantage of new food sources. Always

Continued on next page

assume that grizzlies are in the area and make sure your camps, cabins, and homes are bear proof and that bear attractants are unavailable or contained.

- Carry bear pepper spray. Keep the bear pepper spray within reach and be familiar with the firing mechanism. In sudden grizzly encounters pepper spray has proven to be a valuable deterrent tool. Grizzly bears sprayed in the face at very close range often stop attacking and are less likely to inflict injury.

- Mentally rehearse a worst-case scenario with a grizzly bear. "If the mind has never been there before, the body does not know how to respond."

- As a last resort, if attacked, play dead. Lie face down, covering your neck and head with your hands and arms. If you have a backpack leave it on to protect your back. Stay face down, never look at the bear and remain still until the bear is gone. Many people have survived bear attacks using this method.

Chapter 29

Guided or
Self-Guided Hunts

Warning: Hunting elk is not like hunting deer. You don't typically go out in the back forty and shoot a pair of antlers and steaks for the freezer. Elk are more mobile, far ranging, and willing to go to considerable lengths to avoid you, so hunting elk usually requires more effort than hunting whitetails or even mule deer. You need to be in excellent physical shape to hunt elk, whether you're going with a guide or on your own. And you'll have to put a good deal of thought into planning your trip.

Above all, start your preparations early. A year in advance of a trip is not too soon to begin asking lots of questions, doing research, and becoming well informed. First, decide what you are looking for in a trip. Is going after a trophy or a big-antlered elk your main aim, or are you happy to get a cow elk? What kind of habitat do you want to hunt? And what state are you interested in hunting?

You may know the answers to these questions from the outset, or your desires may change and evolve as you look into various possibilities and learn more about them. But before you get into the details of your planning, have a clear sense of your own expectations for the trip. And if you're going on the trip with other hunters make sure you all have similar goals, or at least goals that are compatible.

Once these basic expectations are clear, you'll have to decide whether to hire an outfitter or tackle the trip on your own. It's a big decision and an important one.

A *good* guide will tell you when and where to apply for necessary licenses and permits and give you a complete list of the clothing and gear you'll need to bring. He'll know the idiosyncrasies of the local terrain, habitats, and game. He'll get you to the best places to hunt at the best times of day given the weather conditions. He'll feed you, wash your dishes, fix you a comfortable place to sleep, and wake you up when it's time to hunt. He'll tell you stories and listen to yours. He'll try all his tricks to get you hooked up with the kind of elk you want to shoot. And if you shoot it, he'll field dress the elk, pack it to camp, and ship it to your home or to the taxidermist.

A *good* guide won't guarantee that you'll shoot a trophy elk or even a cow elk. Getting an elk is just not a sure thing, even with the best of guides. You need to know that from the start.

A *good* guide will also charge you a good amount of money for his services. If you can't afford to pay for such a trip, or are unwilling to let go of that amount of cash, you're left to your own devices. That means you will be responsible for all the things a guide would do for you, in addition to hunting all day. You'll have to chop wood, cook meals, wash dishes, feed the fire all night when it's cold, and keep the tent ropes tight. It can be done; it's just not quite as much fun for some hunters. Are you one of them?

While you're working toward making the guide/self-guide decision, there are some things you should check out on the Internet, which has become one of the best sources for getting up-to-date information for planning a hunting trip. If you don't have a computer with Internet access, most public libraries provide free access. And resource people at the library can help you use a

Guided hunts can be very rewarding, but you need to do your homework first. (Jay Cassell)

search engine like Google or Jeeves to find information if you aren't familiar with computers.

Start your search by typing "state fish and game departments" into your search engine's search box. You'll quickly find several websites that lists these departments alphabetically by state. Each state has its own website containing information on elk seasons, trip planning, rules and regulations, and the cost and due dates for resident and nonresident applications and permits. Most states provide a variety of other useful information, including such things as a list of private and public hunting opportunities, the status of state elk populations, big-game records, tips on planning a hunt, lists of outfitters and guides, and phone numbers where you can get more information if you have questions.

You can also ask Google or Jeeves to search for "elk hunts." That will bring up a list of outfitters who specialize in guided hunts for elk in the U.S. But perhaps the best place to get a feel for what outfitters have to offer is at a sportsmen's show where

Outfitters can take you into elk country in style.

outfitters have booths and you can talk to them in person, ask questions, and get immediate responses.

Whether talking with an outfitter face to face or over the phone, here are some questions you might ask after you've explained what your hopes are for a hunt:

• How many years have you outfitted in your area?

• How many years will my guide have guided in the area?

- What kind of hunting will we be doing—vehicle, horse, foot, or combination?

- How many miles a day will we cover, over what kind of terrain?

- How long is the hunting day?

- How many days will we actually hunt?

- Will we be hunting on public or private land?

- What kind of accommodations and meals do you provide?

- What is the total cost including extra fees, charges, permits, tips, etc.?

- Are there additional fees for a trophy or for shipping meat, hide, or antlers?

- What is your hunter success ratio?

- Are you licensed and insured?

- Are you a member of the state outfitters and guides association?

Ask these questions of at least three outfitters who sound as though they could provide the services you're looking for. Ask each outfitter for a list of references, including some hunters who didn't take any game. Call at least three references provided by each outfitter.

This will be time consuming, but when you're done you'll have a clear idea of which outfitter will best fill your needs, and you can sign on with him. Or you'll know for sure that you can't afford the service and will have to go on your own.

When planning for a self-guided trip, use the Internet resources I've mentioned, plus any other leads you can find, to decide exactly where you want to hunt. Check out possibilities on both public and private land, and make sure hunting access is available to you. Then, call state game managers in the areas you're considering to find out the status of the elk population, especially mature bulls if you're interested in going for a trophy. Also make sure the kind of licenses you want are available for that hunting area.

Once you decide on a specific area, make all necessary applications for licenses, permits, and tags well ahead of their due dates. These vary from year to year and from state to state, with some states posting application deadlines as early as January and other states as late as June.

Once applications are in the mail or sent via Internet, purchase good topographic maps of the area you're planning to hunt, and use them to start to get a good mental picture of the lay of the land and how elk might use it and how you might hunt it.

Next, decide on hunting accommodations. A motel room will pamper you, but you'll have to drive to and from your hunting area each day. That could take valuable time out of the best hunting hours. A camp will put you in or near the heart of good hunting, which is usually preferable to the motel option.

If at all possible, make arrangements to secure a specific camp spot on private or public land, and confirm a reservation for that site. Find out what is provided at the site in the way of water, fire grates, tables, and so forth. Then determine what gear and equipment you'll need to bring to satisfy your expectations for a comfortable camp. Do you need a generator and a wall tent with a wood stove and a portable potty? Or can you be happy with a backpacker's tent and a flashlight?

When sharing the responsibility of providing camp gear and food with other hunters, work with a master list that you can check off. Weeks before you depart on your hunting adventure, take a day to meet with all your hunting buddies with all your gear and provisions. Spread it all out, set it all up, make sure it all works. Check it off your master list. Then pack it up, and make sure it fits in the vehicle you'll be taking. And be sure that vehicle is reliable, recently serviced, and sporting good tires.

And, amid all this planning and equipping, figure out exactly how you will care for, process, store, and transport any game you get once you arrive at your hunting destination. Can you hire a local horsepacker to haul out any elk you get? Is there a local game processor who will handle cutting, wrapping, and shipping meat? Is there a local taxidermist who will mount trophy heads and send them to you?

At this point you may be thinking that you actually can afford the services of that outfitter who really did sound perfect for the hunt you want to take. So it might be appropriate to end this

Horses are a huge help in packing meat and antlers out of the backcountry.

discussion with a look at how one guide views his profession and the clients he serves.

Duaine Hagen, an outfitter out of Cody, Wyoming, has this to say about why he's in the guiding business: "It's the lifestyle. It sure beats sitting behind a desk. And the experience and enjoyment you provide your client is a big reward. I've got clients who live from year to year to come out here."

But Hagen will tell you that guiding has become more than just taking people hunting. "The role has changed for the outfitter and guide. We're not only expected to be good hunters and be able to get clients into game; we have to be naturalists, too. We have to interpret and we have to educate. And we're kind of responsible for the backcountry. So we teach low-impact camping techniques.

"In the past," says Hagen, "there were a lot of guides who had this macho thing where they were going to show the dude how tough they were. Well, those guys don't make it on my place very long. People are not coming out West to see how tough somebody else is. They're out here to have a good time and a good experience and to share it with somebody. It's our job to provide that."

In the process of doing so, guides meet a mixed bag of clients. Many of them make guides glad they're in the business, but some make for long days. These are the clients who don't want to pay attention to the rules, forcing the guide to double as game warden. They're the ones who can't be happy unless they shoot a trophy no matter what, or who expect to be shown a parade of elk as if they were in a theme park, instead of the real forests and alpine meadows of the West. If you're hunting for the right reasons, you won't be one of those dudes. On the other hand, if an outfitter isn't providing the services he promised, he needs to be called on that fact.

STATES AND PROVINCES WITH ELK-HUNTING SEASONS

In the following listing of states and provinces, Arizona, California, Colorado, Idaho, Montana, New Mexico, Oregon, Utah, Washington, and Wyoming have the best elk-hunting opportunities. California currently has only about 10,000 elk, but it's the only state that boasts Roosevelt, Tule, and Rocky Mountain elk. Of the Canadian provinces, British Columbia, with an estimated population of 40,000 elk, holds the most promise, particularly the southeast region. Although other states and provinces offer only limited hunting opportunities, they are all worth considering, especially if you live nearby.

The most comprehensive information from fish and game departments is often available from their websites, so that is where I recommend you start your planning.

UNITED STATES

Alaska Department of Fish and Game
http://www.state.ak.us/adfg
907-465-4190

Arizona Game and Fish Department
http://www.azgfd.gov
602-942-3000

Arkansas Game and Fish Commission*
http://www.agfc.state.ar.us
501-223-6331

California Department of Fish and Game*
http://www.dfg.ca.gov/
916-653-7664

Colorado Department of Natural Resources, Division of Wildlife
http://wildlife.state.co.us
303-291-7299

Idaho Fish and Game Department
http://fishandgame.idaho.gov
208-334-3700

Kansas Department of Wildlife and Parks*
http://www.ink.org/public/kdwp/
913-296-2281

Kentucky Department of Fish and Wildlife Resources
http://www.kdfwr.state.ky.us
502-564-4336

Michigan Department of Natural Resources, Wildlife Division*
http://www.michigan.gov/dnr
517-373-1263

Minnesota Department of Natural Resources*
http://www.dnr.state.mn.us/
612-296-6157

Montana Department of Fish, Wildlife & Parks
http://www.fwp.state.mt.us
406-444-2950

Nebraska Game and Parks Commission*
http://www.ngpc.state.ne.us/
402-471-0641

Nevada Department of Conservation and Natural Resources,
    Division of Wildlife
http://www.nevadadivisionofwildlife.org/
702-688-1500

New Mexico Department of Game and Fish
http://www.wildlife.state.nm.us
505-827-7911

North Dakota State Game and Fish Department*
http://www.state.nd.us/gnf/
701-328-6363

Oklahoma Department of Wildlife Conservation
http://www.wildlifedepartment.com/
405-521-3851

Oregon Department of Fish and Wildlife
http://www.dfw.state.or.us/
503-872-5275

Pennsylvania Department of Conservation and Natural
   Resources, Game Commission
http://www.dcnr.state.pa.us/
717-787-7015

South Dakota Department of Game, Fish and Parks*
http://www.sdgfp.info
605-773-3485

Utah Department of Natural Resources, Division of
   Wildlife Resources
http://www.nr.utah.gov
801-538-4700

Washington Department of Fish and Wildlife
http://wdfw.wa.gov
360-902-2200

Wyoming Game and Fish Department
http://gf.state.wy.us/
307-777-4600

CANADA

Alberta Department of Environmental Protection, Natural
 Resources Services
http://www3.gov.ab.ca/srd/fw/hunting/
463-422-2079

British Columbia Ministry of Environment, Wildlife Branch
250-387-1161

Manitoba Department of Natural Resources*
http://www.gov.mb.ca/environ/index.htm
1-800-214-6497

Saskatchewan Environment and Resources Management,
 Wildlife Division
http://www.gov.sk.ca/
306-787-2314

Resident Permits Only

Chapter 30

BACKPACKING TO
BETTER HUNTING

Unlike most outdoorsmen, I became a hunter by way of back-packing. While many of my friends spent their falls carrying a rifle, I spent that time toting a pack. The potential hunter in me really didn't start to come out until one autumn when I was asked to join a mountain goat hunt. My presence on the trip was more as a Sherpa than a hunter, but the experience taught me that I was in better shape than my companions and as aware of wildlife habits and habitat as they were. So the following year I bought a rifle and was given a short course in firearms, field dressing, and butchery by a friend. Since then I've been a backpacking hunter, and my background of backpacking has paid handsome dividends in the field.

As a backpacker you have several advantages over the average hunter. The time you spend hiking the hills during the summer helps get your legs and lungs in shape for the rigors of the hunting season. In addition, the more time you spend backpacking in the mountains and forests, the more intimately you become acquainted with where the animals are and what to expect of them. When the season opens, a backpacker can get to wherever the game may be

The author began backpacking for elk many years ago.

with a minimum cash outlay. Even if you have a four-wheel-drive vehicle or can afford a horse outfitter, there are many good hunting spots that you'll be able to reach only under your own steam. Besides, the backpacker doesn't have to spend a lot of time commuting to his favorite hunting area. Nor does he have to feel tied down to a hard-to-move base camp.

"There is a catch," you may wryly note. "Once the backpacker gets his eight hundred pounds of trophy elk, he's got to lug the darn thing out, along with the rest of his gear!" There's some weight to that fact, of course. But some basic know-how when it comes to gear, early preparation, and hunting logistics will make backpack hunting easier from start to finish—including getting that load of heavy meat and hide home.

THE GEAR

Of all the backpacks on the market today, the frame pack made of contoured aluminum still remains the only choice for the backpacking hunter. Based on the old wood and canvas Trapper Nelson, the basic frame pack is the only one with a detachable bag. This feature is a must when it comes time to pack out your game.

In selecting a pack, the strength of the frame is extremely important. The standard H type frame will have three to five horizontal crossbars which should be welded in place. Avoid frames that have been brazed, epoxied, or bolted together. A good test for the strength of a frame is to put just one of its legs on the floor and then apply diagonal pressure by leaning on the top of the opposite leg. Any appreciable give means the frame won't hold up well under heavy use.

Other features to look for on a pack include padded shoulder straps and hip belt. In a properly adjusted pack, your hips, not your shoulders, will carry most of the weight, so padding here is really necessary. Found as standard equipment on only a few packs, but available as an accessory for most, is a tubular shelf for the bottom of the frame. This feature will simplify the task of lashing game to your pack and help prevent your load from slipping. It's well worth purchasing.

Boots are next in importance. Even if your pack will handle hefty loads, poorly shod feet can be your downfall—literally. Remember, your favorite hunting boots aren't necessarily built to give you the ankle support needed when carrying a pack. I've found medium-weight hiking boots—about four pounds a pair—to be ideal backpacking/hunting footwear. Cut just above the ankle, these boots have an arch support and inner padding. Their lugged soles offer good traction in steep country and on snow. When using them in snow, knee-high gaiters keep slush out of your boots and prevent your legs from getting damp and cold. Gore-Tex® is preferable to a truly waterproof material for gaiters because it "breathes" and prevents condensation from forming inside next to your legs. Fashion a homemade outer liner of wool or flannel to go over the gaiter if the noise of twigs slapping against it poses a problem while hunting in brushy country.

External-frame packs are the best choice for backpacking hunters. (Cabela's)

Most of the camping equipment you carry should be standard backpacking gear. You'll want a down or polyester sleeping bag with a pad, a two- to four-man nylon tent and extra clothing. Keep your kitchen lightweight by using freeze-dried or dehydrated food and aluminum cookware. A first-aid kit, flashlight, and topographic maps and compass should also be included in your pack. Fifty feet of ⅛-inch cord will serve both your camping needs and as lashing material when it comes to packing out your game.

Before you get your game out, of course, it will have to be field dressed. How you cut it up for carrying will depend on what you have. In most instances you'll at least want to quarter your game.

A good knife and small, light saw are vital for field dressing an elk far from your vehicle. (Cabela's)

With an elk, taking the meat off the bone may be the only reasonable way of packing it out. In any event, you should have along some basic butchering tools that aren't too heavy or bulky. Your hunting knife can be carried on your belt. However, a saw and a hatchet are usually necessary when faced with the task of quartering an animal. For backpack hunting, I've found that a sheath saw about twelve inches long with coarse teeth on one side and fine teeth on the other works well. It's light and compact and fits nicely into a corner of your pack. Likewise, a small hatchet head, designed to be used with a makeshift wooden handle, can be carried on your belt in its sheath or tucked in a pocket of the pack. Neither of these tools will add much to the weight you'll be carrying and will seem worth every ounce after you've downed your game.

There are plenty of books and videos available for learning the basics of field dressing and butchering. One of the best books is *Field Dressing and Butchering Big Game,* by Monte Burch.

EARLY PREPARATION

One of the most enjoyable aspects of backpack hunting is that it can and should take place all year long. Whether hiking in the summer on foot or snowshoeing during the winter months, you should be checking out game concentrations and movements in the areas you plan to hunt in the fall. Noting their daily patterns of movement in the course of feeding, drinking, and resting can help you pinpoint specific locations to position yourself during the hunting season.

Game trails are the best indicators of animal activities. But in addition to clueing you in to the behavior of game, they also provide a path into the heart of good hunting country. During the summer, when manmade hiking trails are often crowded, you can enjoy the solitude of game trails with only the presence of the animals that made them, and you'll discover important things about those animals in the process.

Unless you've spent considerable time on these natural trails, they can appear bewildering on occasion. While traversing steep hillsides or open meadows, trails may disappear suddenly. The reason for this is understandable in the case of open terrain. While in the confines of timber or brush, there is usually one major route of least resistance which all game will take, thus making a clearly defined trail. Once the animals reach open country, however, they are free to meander where they please and the trail becomes indistinct. A quick survey of the surrounding brush or timber, particularly where it provides thick escape cover, will usually reveal another trail.

Trails disappearing on steep hillsides aren't explained as easily. On numerous occasions I've followed distinct paths that petered out in the middle of a hill, and then I've found the trail again at a higher or lower elevation. In observing elk in these locations at a later time, I would see animals traveling single file that suddenly broke off to crisscross haphazardly uphill, only to return to a single file at a higher point. I've never figured out the reason for this behavior, but I've discovered I can usually relocate a trail on a hillside if I head directly up or down from the point it disappeared.

Trails on ridges deserve special attention. These are often routes game will use to move to low ground when autumn storms make things unpleasant in the high country. Shorter tributary routes leading off a main ridgeline path will probably lead to water sources, feeding grounds, and escape cover. A careful check of all these trails in a specific hunting area will give you a good idea of where and when to station yourself in order to have the best chance of observing game.

Then there are trails that wind their way through the timber and break out into ridgeline saddles or passes. A trail like this can be a real find because it's usually a major game route used for crossing from one canyon or drainage into another. It not only provides a backpacking hunter with access to new territory, it also is a prime vantage point for spotting game, particularly when you know heavy hunting pressure in one drainage is likely to push animals into the other.

HUNTING LOGISTICS

The most important aspect of a backpacking hunter's method of operation is setting up specific guidelines for the hunt. Where you make your camp, and the relationship of that camp to your vehicle, to roads in the area, and to the country you plan to cover are all important considerations. To help plan these specifics, before you ever set foot in the woods, study a topographic map of the area. The 7½-minute series (1:24,000 scale) will give you the most detail.

The first concern should be locating your camp. Other than selecting a comfortable location, I've found that it's extremely important to be within easy access of areas that game is likely to frequent during the morning and evening. Watering holes and feeding grounds are likely places, and summer hikes along the game trails in the vicinity should have let you know where these spots can be found. By making camp nearby, you'll be able to hunt these areas at productive times of the day without having to walk very far to get to and from your base of operations.

Ideally, you'll place your camp as near as possible to the center of the territory you plan to cover. The size of that area will depend on the terrain and a variety of other factors, but you should set some specific boundaries at the outset so you don't, in the heat of the hunt, find yourself with fifteen miles of mountains between your downed elk and the nearest road.

You'll have to determine for yourself what is a reasonable area to cover. With elk, you need to factor in that it may take five or six pack loads to get the game out. Only after you know the terrain you'll be in, the number of days you can spend on the hunt, and whether you can get friends to help pack things out will you

When the adrenaline of the shot begins to fade, you realize just how much work lies ahead. Plan accordingly. (Jay Cassell)

be able to set perimeters for your hunting grounds. The important thing is to be realistic about the general boundaries and to stay within them once established.

By setting up some ground rules for yourself, you should be able to avoid that feeling of sheer panic when you finally down the elk you've been after and realize how much work lies ahead. I must admit, however, that every animal I've gotten while backpacking has looked a great deal bigger than the scales indicated upon arriving home. To avoid getting into more than you can handle, sit down and do some figuring once the field-dressing chores are over. Do you have time to pack anything out that day or should you head for camp and wait until morning? How many trips will it take and how long will they be? Can you get someone to help? All these questions should be answered before you decide what to do. Otherwise, you may find yourself crashing through the underbrush in the coal-bin dark or misplacing your camp for the night.

Speaking of losing things, of particular interest to the backpacking hunter is the matter of keeping track of his game once it's down. Even if you have the location of your tent memorized, relocating the elk you shot isn't always as easy. As a prime example, take the plight of an Ohio hunter who came to hunt on national forest land near my home. The fellow was lucky enough to bag an excellent (and very large) animal, but with dusk approaching, he decided to leave the job of packing it out until the following day. That evening he telephoned his good news home to family and friends and made plans for the next morning. Unfortunately, it snowed during the night. Nothing looked the same in the forest upon his return. Landmarks he'd noted were buried or so transformed they were unrecognizable. As a result, he returned home with nothing and was forced to endure the ribbing of his friends when he talked about his trophy. To avoid such a misfortune, make sure you take compass readings on the spot you down your animal. A red bandana tied to the under branches of a nearby tree can help too, particularly when snow may have covered the game.

There are a few final concerns when it comes to winding up your backpack hunting trip successfully. First, remember that a set of antlers bobbing through the forest on the back of a pack may look very much like a live animal. To guard against having rifles pointed your way, it's wise to hang antlers upside down from your pack frame. A colorful article of clothing hung on the rack adds even a bit more insurance. Second, the last load packed out of the woods should be reserved for your camping gear. It's convenient to be able to brew up a hot cup of coffee or a hot lunch in camp when the weather's cold and you still have more game to pack out. But you never can tell when it will be more than a convenience. If a sudden storm should come up or an accident occur, your camp provides a real haven, particularly in the remote and seldom traveled country to which the backpacking hunter has access.

WHAT TO MAKE OF AN ELK

Among many of the Indian cultures of North America hunting elk for food was secondary to the uses elk served in making clothing, shelter, weapons, tools, and innumerable other "household" items. In fact, there was hardly any part of an elk that wasn't used for some important aspect of an Indian's material or spiritual life.

For many tribes elk-skin blankets had specific standards of value against which trade items were appraised. Explorers Lewis and Clark, for example, had to depart with a rifle to get two elk-skin blankets, and they gave up two canoes for four elk-skin blankets and two robes.

But mostly Indians made a living out of elk. Here are some of the ways.

Hide: bags, ropes, dresses, shirts, leggings, tipi covers, moccasins, shields, armor, harnesses, bedding, belts, ceremonial mats, rifle scabbards, quiver linings, glue, boats, canoes, artist's canvas

Antlers: hooks, bows, spears, harpoons, gaffs, knives, clubs, saddle frames, wedges, chisels, adzes, spoons, handles, picks, fleshers, scrapers, headdresses, pestles

Bones: food, grease, dyes, salves, awls, needles, forks, chisel points, arrow points, handles, drawblades, knives, fleshers, hoes, scrapers, harpoon points, club handles

Teeth: beads, pendants, necklaces, earrings, charms

Hooves: glue

Brain: tanning agent, food

Continued on next page

Eyes, tongue, heart, lungs, intestines, liver, kidneys, testicles, blood, muscles: food
Hair: ornaments, embroidery
Sinew: string, thread
Fecal matter: fertilizer, tobacco
Stomach/bladder: bags

Chapter 31

ELK CAMP

There's a reasonable explanation for hunting camps in country as immense as the Rockies: You have to be near those wily elk when they nose out of the timber at dusk and spirit back through the trees come dawn. It's no fun hauling horses back and forth to town over rutted, pot-holed roads every morning and every night. You have to be out there when the weather works its white magic to bring elk down from alpine basins and windswept ridges.

It only makes sense.

Then there's the real reason. Hunting camps are a Western social tradition, a cultural artifact from a time when a tent was the shelter of necessity and choice for loggers, miners, and trappers, a makeshift place to poke chapped hands up to a barrel stove that's ticking and cherry-red with heat, where camp coffee brews and tall talk eddies with the smell of canvas like a good fishing hole in a creek.

Sometimes gun-toting girlfriends and determined wives come along, but hunting camps are mainly a gathering of men: brothers, brother-in-laws, cousins, sons, often a handful of close friends.

It starts with a couple of guys with wall tents from Montana Canvas, or Blue Star, or maybe Army surplus—one tent for cooking, one for sleeping. Then another guy has a stove, a 55-gallon drum he's chopped off and propped up with his welding torch. Someone else throws in Coleman lanterns and cots. Four or five of them pool their personal gear to make it all come together in a comfortable camp.

Some cold day, knock on the tent flap of a drive-in hunting camp like Bob Arrotta's, and you'll chuckle when you're welcomed into the surprising warmth. Carpets on the ground. Tables and chairs. A full-sized kitchen stove converted to propane, something to cook Thanksgiving dinner, turkey and all—and it has, Bob will tell you.

Then check out the camp down the creek, those guys from Colstrip, Montana, who've commuted the four hundred miles round trip to hunt elk the last ten years. One of them thought a bathtub might improve the place so he whacked a steel drum in half. Two buckets of water from their wood-fired water heater and two buckets from a hole chopped in the ice-bound stream make an ease-in bath, as long as you remember to wedge the tub with firewood so it won't roll.

But amid the carpets, stoves, and tubs, there's no lack of rustic: tent poles with limb stubs left for hanging coats and cups. Mitten-drying racks made up from branches of lodgepole pine. They're an eclectic blend of store-bought, castoff, and make-do, these drive-in hunting camps.

Some guys go more basic—a horse trailer swept out and installed with a stove. Others, like Mark Matheny, find a piece of private land to build a tree camp twelve feet off the ground with rugs over the pole floor, a picture window by the kitchen table, built-in bunks, and a deck that overlooks ridges where elk feed. The ultimate tree stand.

The camp you pack in on horses is more Spartan: the wall tent with fresh patches where last year a grizzly went through, the knock-down wood stove with water jacket, the grub box, the bedrolls. All packed in panniers and tied down with diamond hitches and led off on a string of horses to the same place you've gone for years.

Location is much of what makes a camp. A landscape storied with names like Wapiti Meadows, Blizzard Ridge, Dead Horse Creek, Sunlight Basin, Expedition Pass, Raw Liver Creek, Cowboy Heaven. Who isn't lured by names like that?

A hunting camp is right out there in the cold, and the wind, and the snow. It's there where the cow moose and her calf hang out near your tent to mooch hay from the horses. It's there where coyotes yap at their own echoes and wind pushes against the night. Where you keep the toilet seat stashed by the stove until you really have to go at thirty below.

"For elk hunting, the best time to be there's when it's down below zero," says Gene Surber, who has been hunting out of a camp for more than twenty-five years. "We don't have any problem

Hunting camps can be as simple or sophisticated as you're willing to make them—just don't forget that you're there to hunt elk.

staying warm. If you're mentally prepared for cold weather, you can relax with it a bit. I've seen it happen over the years with new people to the area. They just freeze to death up there for no reason. I think it's more a fear of the cold than trying to get along with it."

And "getting along with" applies to hunting companions as well as the weather. "We divide up the camp chores—cooking, doing dishes, getting wood," Surber says. "And anyone who doesn't pitch in doesn't ever come back. We've had it happen occasionally. A person will come in and just kind of eat and disappear. But the idea behind hunting camp is the social atmosphere, the friendships we develop. There'll be a number of days we may not even go hunting. You get up in the morning and maybe somebody'll suggest playing cards. And the next thing you know it's the middle of the afternoon. That's the fun part about the camp."

That and the stories. Although fun isn't the word for the story about the time somebody shot Surber's horse.

"It was a buckskin horse tied to a tree with two other horses. Snowing real heavy, snowed about fifteen inches that morning. You couldn't see more than forty or fifty feet. It was a beautiful morning with great big flakes. My boys and I were out hunting. We made a loop down through the timber, and when we came back, there she was on the ground, dead."

He never found out who did it.

Then there was the time he and a friend packed fifteen miles into the Bob Marshall on a grizzly bear hunt many years ago.

"Just after we got camp set up it started to snow, and it snowed real heavy for four days. That tested our air by the time we were done. We just couldn't see, and it just kept snowing. We were way back in, right up against the Continental Divide.

"On the last day of the storm a guy from the University of Wyoming rode into camp. He'd heard that we had a grizzly permit and he'd been tracking this bear for years. So he come into camp and just begged and pleaded with us, saying 'Don't shoot my bear. I've followed that bear from Utah to Montana and I just don't want you shooting my bear.' He had his monitor there on the horse with him so he knew the bear was right there with us.

"Kind of deflates you a little bit when someone sits there and almost cries asking you not to shoot his bear."

They didn't.

So how much *is* hunting a part of hunting camp?

"I'm to the point where I'd almost just enjoy taking a video camera and hunting with that," says Surber.

Hunting camp?

Gene grins. "It's a male bonding thing. That's what my wife tells me."

INDEX